The National Poetry Series was established in 1978 to ensure the publication of five collections of poetry annually through five participating publishers. The series is funded annually by Academy of American Poets / Amazon Literary Partnership, William Geoffrey Beattie, the Gettinger Family Foundation, Bruce Gibney, Tabitha and Stephen King Foundation, Anna and Olafur Olafsson, Penguin Random House, the Poetry Foundation, Gil Schwartz Foundation, and the National Poetry Series Board of Directors.

2024 COMPETITION WINNERS

Games for Children by Keith S. Wilson
Chosen by Rosalie Moffett for Milkweed Editions

82nd Division by D. M. Aderibigbe
Chosen by Colin Channer for Akashic Books

Our Hands Hold Violence by Kieron Walquist
Chosen by Brenda Hillman for Beacon Press

Blue Loop by AJ White
Chosen by Chelsea Dingman for University of Georgia Press

Shade Is a Place by MaKshya Tolbert
Chosen by Maggie Millner for Penguin

GAMES for CHILDREN

GAMES for CHILDREN

poems

KEITH S. WILSON

MILKWEED EDITIONS

© 2025, Text by Keith S. Wilson
All rights reserved. Except for brief quotations in critical articles or reviews, no part of this book may be reproduced in any manner without prior written permission from the publisher: Milkweed Editions, 1011 Washington Avenue South, Suite 300, Minneapolis, Minnesota 55415. (800) 520-6455
milkweed.org

Published 2025 by Milkweed Editions
Printed in Canada
Cover design by Alex Guerra
25 26 27 28 29   5 4 3 2 1
First Edition

Library of Congress Cataloging-in-Publication Data
Names: Wilson, Keith S. author
Title: Games for children : poems / Keith S. Wilson.
Description: First edition. | Minneapolis, Minnesota : Milkweed Editions, 2025. | Winner of the National Poetry Series; selected by Rosalie Moffett | Summary: "Thematically expansive and materially ambidextrous, the collection of poetry demonstrates how play is one of the highest forms of freedom"-- Provided by publisher.
Identifiers: LCCN 2025007034 (print) | LCCN 2025007035 (ebook) | ISBN 9781639551279 trade paperback | ISBN 9781639551309 ebook
Subjects: LCGFT: Poetry
Classification: LCC PS3623.I585435 G36 2025 (print) | LCC PS3623.I585435 (ebook) | DDC 811/.6--dc23/eng/20250228
LC record available at https://lccn.loc.gov/2025007034
LC ebook record available at https://lccn.loc.gov/2025007035

Milkweed Editions is committed to ecological stewardship. We strive to align our book production practices with this principle, and to reduce the impact of our operations in the environment. We are a member of the Green Press Initiative, a nonprofit coalition of publishers, manufacturers, and authors working to protect the world's endangered forests and conserve natural resources. *Games for Children* was printed on acid-free 100% postconsumer-waste paper by Friesens Corporation.

CONTENTS

A TRANSCENDENTAL FUNCTION 1

MEMORIAL 2

THE INVITATION 3

UNCANNY EMMETT TILL 6

EXIT INTERVIEW 8

LINE DANCE FOR AN AMERICAN TEXTBOOK 14

APOTHEOSIS 20

VIRGIN AND CHILD IN MAJESTY SURROUNDED BY SIX ANGELS 21

MELTING POT 22

ANGEL FOOD 24

PROCESSING EMMETT TILL 26

SEVERAL DEFINITIONS OF "PLAY" IN WHICH I NEVER SAY THE WORD ONCE 28

ANGLES OF INCIDENCE 38

ON WONDER 39

TO THE GIRL(S) THAT DATED ME TO UNRAVEL THEIR WHITE FATHER 41

TO THE WARMTH A BELLY MAKES WHEN SPARE AGAINST ANOTHER BELLY 41

THERE AREN'T ENOUGH IDIOMS ABOUT THE STARS 42

SPELL TO TRACE A RAINBOW TO ITS APOGEE 44

BATTER BREAD, MULATTO STYLE (1935) 45

THERE'S A CONCEPT CALLED CHRONOSTASIS 46

THE UNCANNY PUMP FAKE 49

MUSE 52

SONNET (BROWN) 54

WHAT PHOENIX LEARNS IN PASSING 56

FEAR OF DOORS 59

LEGEND 63

GERRYMANDER FOR A BLACK SENTENCE 64

APOTHEOSIS 65

A TRANSLATION   67

SELF-PORTRAIT AS A BIRD THROUGH GLASS   68

CAPTION   69

BLUEPRINT FOR A PRISON DEATH BED   71

THE GAMBLER   72

SUBJUNCTIVE EMMETT TILL   75

TENSES   76

THINGS I'VE FOUND LEFT IN THIS FIELD   77

WALMART   78

UNDERGOD   80

SEED   81

BONUS ACTIVITY   82

APOTHEOSIS   83

AP·PRE·HEN·SION   84

SERAPHIM   85

AMERICAN LYRIC   88

WAILING MAP   90

LANDSCAPE WITH MONA LISA   91

UNCANNY COLUMBINE   93

SEED   94

WE WERE MADE TO PLAY IN THE WHOLENESS OF THE FIELD   96

SOMETHING CAST FROM BRONZE   97

FIELD SWITCH   98

WHO IS THERE TO EULOGIZE THE TREE   100

MIDSUMMER   102

{   104

NOTES   105

SOURCES   121

ACKNOWLEDGMENTS   129

History is what hurts. —FREDRIC JAMESON

GAMES for CHILDREN

A TRANSCENDENTAL FUNCTION

in the quiet i hear
my father's voice anesthetized

he babbled to someone:

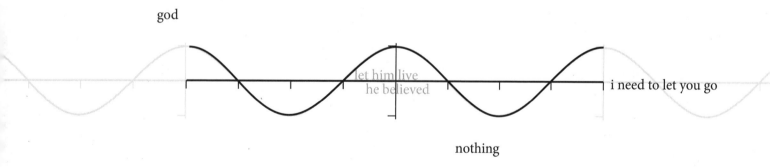

god

let him live
he believed

i need to let you go

nothing

MEMORIAL

We're just simply saying mark the place where it began. —ANN CHINN[*]

when i was born the pipes froze white.
      i edged to midnight but didn't step over.
they were already married. my father and my mother.
playing cards. my name was to be winter.
the ceiling up against the sky.
10 years before they were married,
they could never have married.
when my father saw my body, he gave his name.
in mississippi where the wooden ships came.
water sat warm in every pot.

THE INVITATION

the thing about the scorpion is he built
from his nothing frogsong:

a living song. the story as we tell it
ends sooner than it has to end. consider: the poison
sits like a child in the boiling water of the back: the frog
yells this or that (he moralizes) and is sure to die
and then we go to bed. but before it makes the news,

the frog turned over, sunny-side up. then
the scorpion licked his stomach (sharp, if you take
what i mean). then the frog swallowed
flywater. the scorpion thought this

is it! this is really it! square across
the river like the origin of geometry.

and what of the exoskeleton? was anything beneath it?
only the strange fluid of a different myth.
and do you think the scorpion dared to dream? ah, but he built from nothing

frogdance (a flopping). oh to be so loud,
to touch the thigh
and the cheek and the inner part of the eye
that is sharp-

tongued and quick to be happy or wide.
to be engorged in the other's orbit, on either side

of history. we might tell
any sort of tale of the water where the dead choose
to go. we might call it anything

to save ourselves the trouble. a hoodwink or a hellish thing.
maryland, or kentucky,

or any border state. delaware. here and there and so on. and again. and then
even the scorpion tasted the water.
he lifted up as if about to drown
and struck again and again and again but the frog

was in another country,
deep below him, in the thickest

part of the story
and the daylight
and the water. it all seemed done as done.

then he dotted his i so he could fully say it. i. i. i. i.
then he too crossed the water

UNCANNY EMMETT TILL

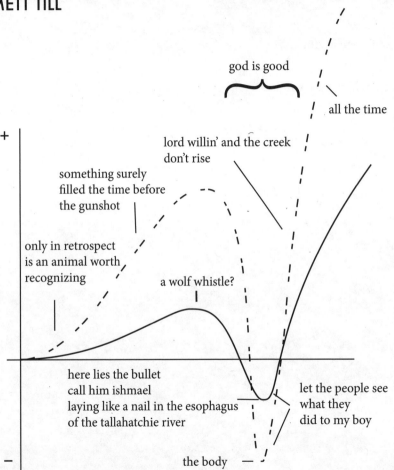

boy	- ..
a world	——

EXIT INTERVIEW

along an autumn bypass just before the sky, you walked
from one job to another—a table of men
assured you they were sorry. there is nothing

they can do. the grass was stiff
and unburdened with snow or water. and the weathervanes.

and then you saw the deer.

there, along the trees.
he limped away—he was just ahead—
and as he led he looked over

and over.

whatever wonder you might've thought
was happening, you saw, instead, was just your heart,
or imagination, or the little difference
between them.

there had been an accident, started well before you

had arrived. now, he was afraid and he meant
only to escape with what was left of him, one antler weeping low like a rope.
you remember no sound or smell
or sense. only the deer and you

walking. you would take a step, and so would he,

but harder. you thought you looked behind you, as if to move
from nothing's path. there were no cars,
no signs of cars, no family,
no deer. often, cruelty means to look away

but sometimes instead the proper name
for this is mercy—you wanted nothing
from this deer but that,

if it had to suffer, it should suffer
in a place you'd left behind. you walked on
and he walked on. his way was certain:
to make of the unbearable

a life—you took some steps forward and he remained just that many
ahead. without trying, you had his eyes
trained on your eyes, and he carried himself

onward like a spring stretched just beyond its means.
as if this were a chase
instead of a coincidence. but what could you say?
in the end you stayed

with him. it was the opposite decision you made
in the city years later
seeing a stranger have a seizure on the street. a man
was already there. he held
his phone against his face. to keep walking, you thought, is no different
than to pray, so maybe both are happening. later,

you are telling someone else about the deer
and they say it is a mistake
to think of it as human. a pathetic fallacy. but you do it here,
not because a deer is human,
but because you are. you don't remember
being in pain, though what else could you be?

the deer is stumbling and all the time you think:
does anything you have the power to do
change this? what if, whatever your choice,

you should see him some day, on a road,
his single antler, a sunrise,
his body enlivening every ordinary brown
just by his having made it. or what if, instead, he should die?
you would never know anything
except that you were late. instead,

you walked on, as if mistakenly, forcing him
to make his body work
to keep working. you like not to think

in order to think

you have no body or mind,
but even before you got here
you had been feeling everything
you knew how to feel in your eyes. besides,

it was much too cold to go some other way (where would you find it?)
and too late (what would you say?). instead, you scraped
on (now you do remember snow), the distance carrying you,
and he turned a dozen more times, probably wondering:

could you do it, could you reach him? yes
maybe. if only he were a man. then

you would leave him be. whatever he thought, your walking
forced him to walk. until finally he saw his way.

he found an opening and stumbled into the white trees, pressing his side

tight against them. not once while you were looking did he ever stop
filling the air with the shape of his body. he watched you pass. he seemed

only to exhale, but that, of course, is impossible.
you hesitated as if to make some excuse
but not long enough
to see his jarful of rubies—you'll remember this—

that to make a better sign of him
you forced yourself
to look away. how time didn't matter.
how it might have been day
or night or your anniversary.
any season. you would always have made it here alone,

your feet and your body
and your thought

of moving forward (you tell yourself
not away). your making
the distinction. how to you, every movement,
to be a movement
is always against the wind.
how it feels to thrum
so long that you are living there,
hands out, near enough to touch
yet never touch—not feeling

by the dark, in the dark—not feeling
at all—but somehow
by your movement, knowing.

LINE DANCE FOR AN AMERICAN TEXTBOOK

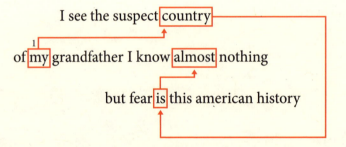

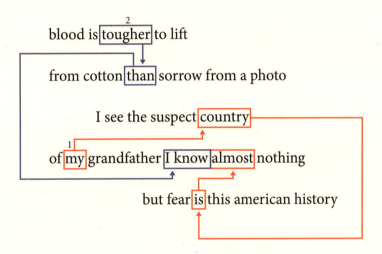

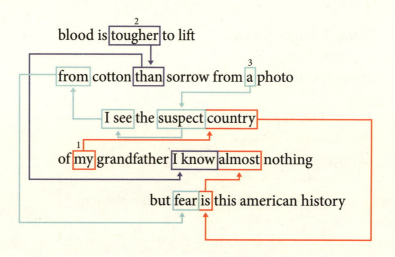

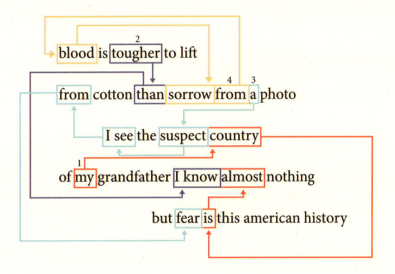

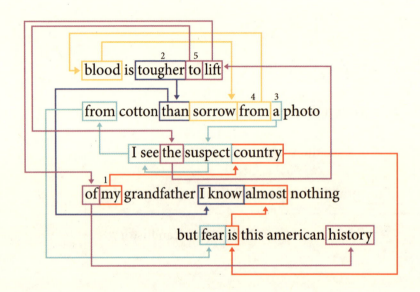

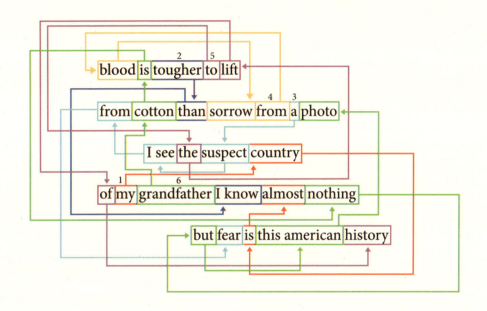

APOTHEOSIS

                          once upon a time, there was a boy

              who struck another boy in the back of his head with a baseball bat—

         he did it without thinking, from a slow-moving car.

              patriot songs—the star-spangled banner, the nfl theme—are national nursery rhymes.

    another term for firecracker is "salute" though a salute can be any number of explosive devices meant to bang.

my palms are bloody lotus pods. a hand appears and a voice sings out: you good? always both: i am and i'm not.

           hot potato treats the potato, the bomb,

and the bean bag as if they weigh the same.

    any coward can hold a lighter but have you held the m80? ready, he says, get set, he says, then off we go.

but am i saying that i understand? he meant it as a joke—his friend walking to the store.

once i closed my eyes to see how long i could drive without dying.

                     i ask: who was he. dad and i go up to pay, wiping our hands on our pants

          in the exact same way.

        no one, he says. a friend of a friend. a boy—a young man—

                        runs out the door—a car alarm going off.

                                      for an instant, i consider running after him

VIRGIN AND CHILD IN MAJESTY SURROUNDED BY SIX ANGELS

do you notice too that all the angels have the same face?
it isn't me. all those faces. it isn't me. once when i was very young

i spent saturday night at a friend's house and was taken
to sunday school. i never had more than one friend.

everyone with jesus in their heart was to stand. i hated suddenly
being reminded of my heart. i could have been made

in that moment to feel anything, the six same-faced angels already
under my hand when pledging my allegiance, whatever the words in me,

this baby jesus looking so much like a man
i could not see myself become, this mary who i knew

nothing about. in my home, when we sat down for dinner,
we ate before an actual woman. at school i was in trouble

for thumping a wet towel over and over against a wall (to hear the sound).
when i rode the bus, i would not look them in the face when they called me

what they called me. i looked out the window.
i stood up.

by the end of it i was saved. did you know i once wore a cross?
in high school. do you remember? i remember almost

all of them

MELTING POT

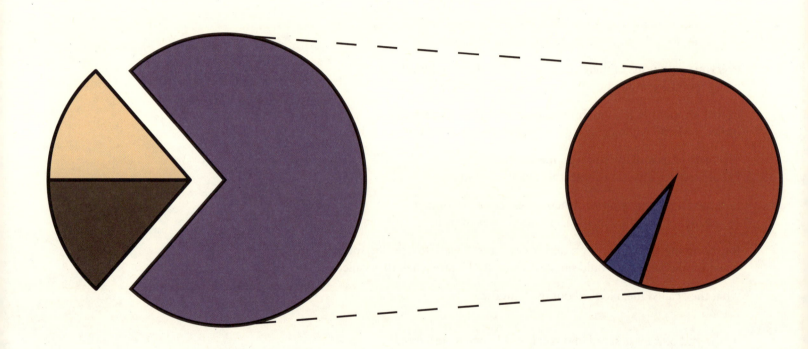

▫ mom removed her makeup, the diner
apron, and made three completely different meals,
every meal. she ate hers last—
just as we finished our glasses
and bowls. she is absent from photos
(a note: daguerreotype was hazy and slow,
and to preserve their children who might die
from the vagaries of victorian life, victorian
mothers would hold their shoulders to keep them
still for the whole of the long exposure.
the women wear a black veil, eclipsed
from the photos or positioned behind a chair,
not sitting. they are called hidden
mothers). once i snapped at her and she started
to cry and even my quiet felt powerful
in a way that made me want to cry myself,
as if both our silences were my own.

▪ my father played dominoes
online, and rather than wonder
at his skill, know that dad is black
and only getting older. he'd become a celebrity
in the leaderboards, and then change
his name. dozens of times, over and over;
no one wants to wrestle a god. the story of america
is a black body reincarnating up and down a ladder
until it runs out of names. my father's father
was a cop. brain cancer took him.

that's the story of justice in america.
dominoes is not so much a game of chance
as one of honor. i was never any good. another fact:
an audience of black and white faces,
in dominoes, is a boneyard. in the end, dad's name
would always betray him. his opponents would recognize
the odds. to save time, he began
naming himself any random word.
he'd dash a career then raise it back up
in the course of days. inheritance ruins bones
(american homes) and so he left it all behind.
constellated_happenstance. revolution83.
some words seem to strangers
like women's names. ivory4. my father,
was the cipher of a man, always silent. but if he won
as a sweet flavor or a tree, magnolia21,
somesummerbreeze, they spoke
and let him know: now, he had always been a bitch.

▪ i fell apart in public once.
         our anniversary.
the waiter didn't notice, or pretended.
the food was fine.

▪ when it comes to a woman undone,
any number of suns might erupt. or none.

ANGEL FOOD

INGREDIENTS
- bitter herbs of the earth
- honey
- evaporated milk
- windfall (apple, persimmon, avocado, pear)
- flour (any spelling)

DIRECTIONS

1. take pains as i did to love
    god like a soul awakened by disaster
2. remember how you were carried
    when you were weak
    [whose hands were that]
3. imagine the hell of a downy thing
    downed by winter
      the wax paper
      of twitchy leaves
4. know you never need to be told to hold yourself
    [like this] against the wind
5. read the history: western philosophy
    was preserved in the honey of arabic
6. find yourself in bed
    [whose hands]
7. promise me if ever i cannot tell you who i am
      (infinity is terrible to the trapped mouse)
    it is over
8. love pull the plug
    from the space heater
      orange foxes
          and crows and almost fire
9. surround us

PROCESSING EMMETT TILL

It is hard to be a god, the door of death closed to me, my grief goes on immortal for ever.
—OVID, "Metamorphoses"

They had probably left it open, as is the custom in homes where a great misfortune has occurred.
—FRANZ KAFKA, *The Metamorphosis*

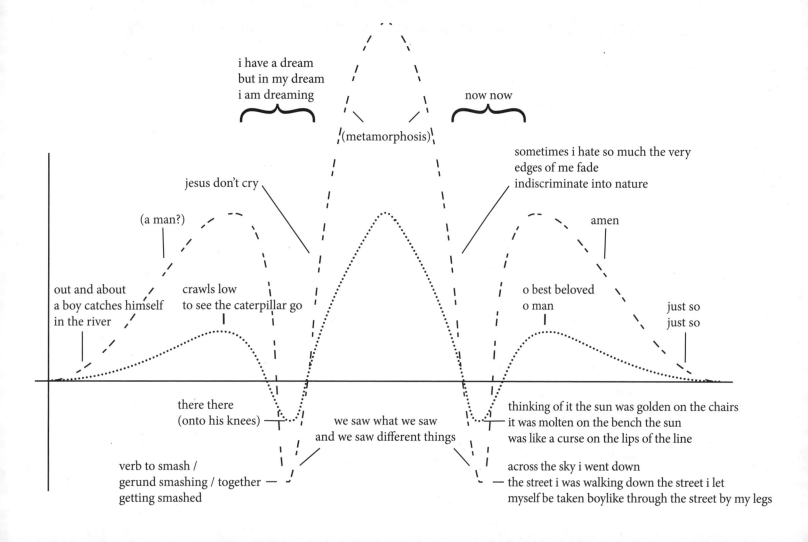

SEVERAL DEFINITIONS OF "PLAY" IN WHICH I NEVER SAY THE WORD ONCE

        i

i am thinking now of evening
the time we had meant to see a show

we were dressed and i ended it
before it began

        really i was thinking of spoiling
        the concept i mean

        how often

        possibility curdled or bloomed
        not by what i said
        but by what i didn't

by way of indirection:

see how
to the practiced hand
music is always too an act of refusal:

first the availability of an action
then the decision not to take it

so that when a song is performed
what you are hearing
is the lyre working in concert
with every song not being made

                ii

a spoiler is that which ruins

say one takes principally for oneself
what was designed to be shared—

that is a spoiler in its broadest sense

    now looking back i see
    how when i say "one" to you
    i mean only me

or put another way if there is a plot
and you betray the fulcrum about which moves that

plot—something

akin to my telling you
as you read alone in bed:

that in the second scene of the second act the thane will be convinced

to act—what good is it to spectate anymore

what good is it
now that we know for sure the future

it is spoiled
there is no sport in that

i didn't say any of this of course—i don't know that i know what
i said

               iii

when i think of the night i think of that night

      take the light on the water
      it is lovely

      when it's lovely

      by the unpredictable pattern of its moving

it works the way we used to work

      when we watched the river cower
      under the trees

      you knew and i didn't know
      you would leave and someday spoil
      your children here

so in the way that light can neither be guided nor guessed at
not at least on moving water
not the light nor to some extent the leaves

which were lovely and must be lovely still

so too could each of us be happy in turbulence

      it is a long way in me getting to another thing
      i was thinking reading the actor's names

      how

      the paradox of plot is that you think you want to know
      but you do not want it
all at once

i think this must be why
to plot
is to engage in trickery

despite all of this
or maybe because of it
every story

to be a story must hide or deceive

it intends to some degree
to fiddle

means to keep you hooked:

      a boy loses his lover and retrieves her

only to abandon her without thinking
that's what he's done

he does it because he believes his tricks
can only culminate in his being tricked back

    our myths are full of this
    but even ordinary men are capable

    of telling a story further than it is meant to be said

        iv

orpheus that is
what if i told you

that that

is an example of a spoiler
not my telling you what happens

i know you know the plot

i mean the looking back

v

another thing susceptible to ruin
is fruit

as in the fresh strawberries
are not anymore

they have been acted upon

by time
that is the spoiler in this case
or every case

    we know that

    time is the maker of the strawberry too
    which maketh of dirt a jewel
    first too bitter to eat and then suddenly

    too soft

which is to say
the true ruiner is impatience

or taste

that i have my hand here upon it

speaking the language of children
because whatever you are now
hitherto we were kids

and so you must remember how once upon a time

every rule

was the beginning of a game i want you to know

i made it
through the field i made it
up the hill i thought

this is finally the place i call

out oxen free

everything is always smaller than one recalls

i put my weight against the tree
imagining i might move it
or barring that
that it might echo and instead move me

ANGLES OF INCIDENCE

Antron McCray •

• Raymond Santana   • Kevin Richardson

• Yusef Salaam

Korey Wise

•

the body is a haunt and non-euclidean
parallel paths will meet

by

110th &
5th

Trisha Meili

a holy name

is a tree growing down the block

& what does it take
to turn an angle
to a blade

is it the moon to you

sparrow's eye

is the other side dark
& small as the trouble it would take

a walk

& if you could
what might you

a jog

an epiphany

84th &
5th   nothing

see

ON WONDER

i try very long walks. very long walks
are a wonder. hunger
too. thirst and other good,
contrasting pains.
when my father hungers
it is an agony. the scar tissue
in his stomach is historical,
meaning it happened in the past
and won't stop happening.
there is a way in which it is a wonder
too. how he lives
wanting to live.
i would not. cannot.
i think it all the time.
crying, every day,
is a betrayal of wonder.
or not crying.
he gave me his name,
and i haven't answered
it yet. the one thing your direct ancestors

have in common is that they lived
(long enough to have children).
there might be nothing else.
i endeavor to be grateful. i try tasting
new things. sometimes the drink
is bitter or the bruises on my feet
are green like spring
or grey also like spring—
in the way of very old pennies
(the kind my father bends down
to get, every time), skin that is blue
like the music or black
like the music too

TO THE GIRL(S) THAT DATED ME TO UNRAVEL THEIR WHITE FATHER

TO THE WARMTH A BELLY MAKES WHEN SPARE AGAINST ANOTHER BELLY

parenthetical heart to parenthetical heart

we waltz—practice touching .... as if to forbear
the oh-so-deliberate astronautical way   our trembling

love is terrible for waiting it grows

..... small as the water earned
we are   from a wound

the inside where the heart should beat
the steady terrible loud beat of a heart

i want to afford you a place
in the stars

the heisenberg uncertainty principle
as i understand it means
you cannot know the speed
at which you must leave
as well as your position

i say this to

the sun —— the sun is the little one to me

to whom i know must go

unbuttoned—not a color
but a wonder

but to the remainder to the moon—i love you
i love you i love you

so what i think

the autumn leaves spilling like a chest
of red linens on red linens

move on

every night

each feverish cup
holding the breadth of water

i

steam the left-
we .... over greens   tonight doesn't need its ribs

let the sun make of the sky
a cavalcade of complicated pinks

once a taxi driver asks outright—what religion
do you practice—as if there were an instrument

what do you suppose is the tone you get from

playing   —   god's empty sheath

call it negative capability—my old-fashioned dreaming

o defeat o roller coasters o bowling alley
o home—four places (sad to go alone)

o sunflower and the tree—

41

THERE AREN'T ENOUGH IDIOMS ABOUT THE STARS

i think a good one would be:
the sky is petty enough without us
pestering it for stars. or, relatedly:
a good star is hard to find. or somehow
under an orange rind you'll rustle up a star. or: betelgeuse
is a hell of a way to spend a night. or
better a cluster of stars than another bad sleep.
you cannot dream with your mouth
open and catch the light of the right star.
if you stretch across a bed you will find the light
of it still across your arm like lotion.
if i exaggerate and call attention to nothing,
it is because as of late, i've become
a hard star out of focus. to catasterize, to place
among the stars, is to curse a foe with darkest ink.
imagine the galaxy as a fable of spilled milk. picture
wanting lemonade. i suppose some of these

are more idioms of space. a shame that any time of year,
whatever you are feeling, the sky at night
remains the same. or what i mean to say is i'm never sure
the season, but yes, i dream of her.

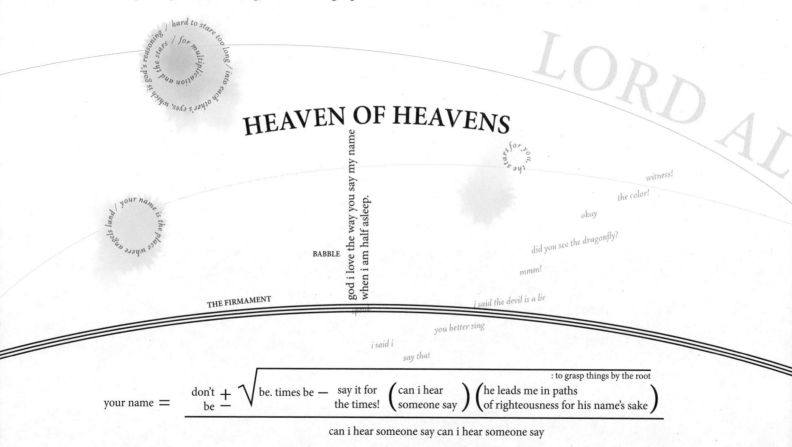

BATTER BREAD, MULATTO STYLE (1935)

we cannot help but be here—
        progress being as it is

a matter of taste. we, whose bodies
        are salty and decemberish

darken under measured reason.
        what reason?

we didn't sit at the table
        but the heat of it raised us.

DIRECTIONS
1. Mix the cold hominy, beaten egg, corn meal and salt with enough boiling water to make a batter of the consistency of milk.
2. Put the lard in a deep baking pan and heat until it smokes.
3. Pour into this hot lard the cold batter; the melted lard will bubble up on the side of the pan, making a delicious crust.
4. Bake in a moderate oven (350°F) about forty minutes.

        enough

like when i cried in the park,
and you did not. the air
was very serious.

you had decided it was over
and i had thought, this is all i have.
once you had gone i began to gather myself

up when i saw somehow the leaves
were growing again from the trees.
you don't understand until you bear it

how perfect memories can be.
i wanted green. i thought
what was your favorite color—blue.

statistically it was blue.

THERE'S A CONCEPT CALLED CHRONOSTASIS

you feel when you first observe
a stimulus—

it causes time
to hang, to hang

or congeal, the way your car does
leaving the road

as you sleep, the way your niece,
your uncertainty, as she is handed

from the nurse
to her father. then you see

her breathe. and him. and then.
and when

you examine a second hand,
it'll seem to take 2 or 3

instances to move (you can stop
and try it now)—now

and then, feeling nothing, i wonder
how actors make themselves cry.

a friend says she pictures her daughter
being hurt, remembers she will never see her son.

i'm not strong enough
a dreamer. every night i chase my sadness down

a couch. in the way of a hawk
marveling at the edge

of the ocean—the ocean that doesn't even have to try.
i told you once

i must be the second person to feel the way i feel
about it. only afraid.

before me was whoever first found salt water equally
in their hands and mouth

and eyes. it is not even about sadness:
sometimes i am happy. and then

nothing. another way
at the illusion is to switch a phone from ear

to ear as you listen
to a sound: time

will cinch your heart to your tongue. i've considered it.
if time heals all wounds, it is because

oblivion is not an opening. i am old enough to know
you can pardon yourself

from one kind of death for another
by going back and forth. forever.

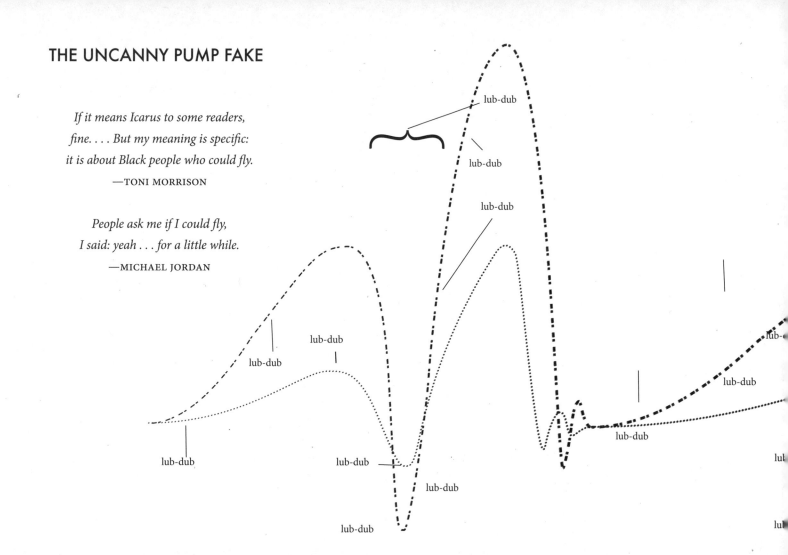

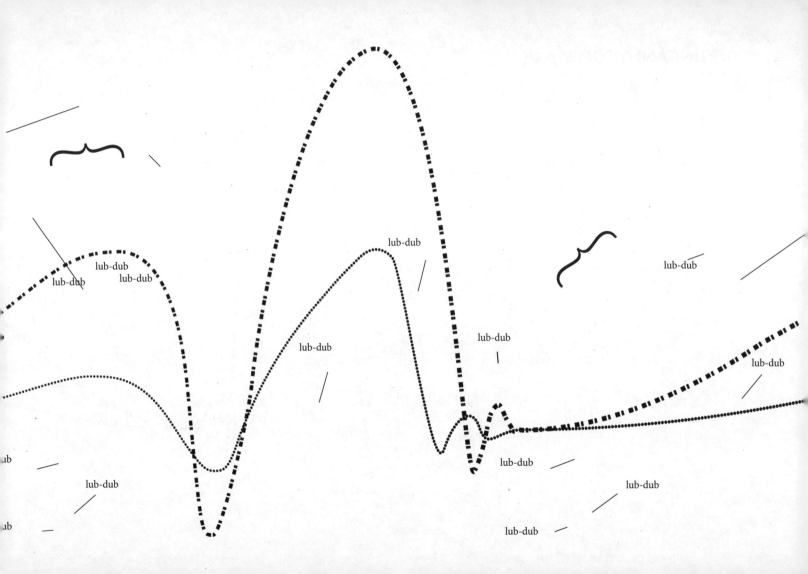

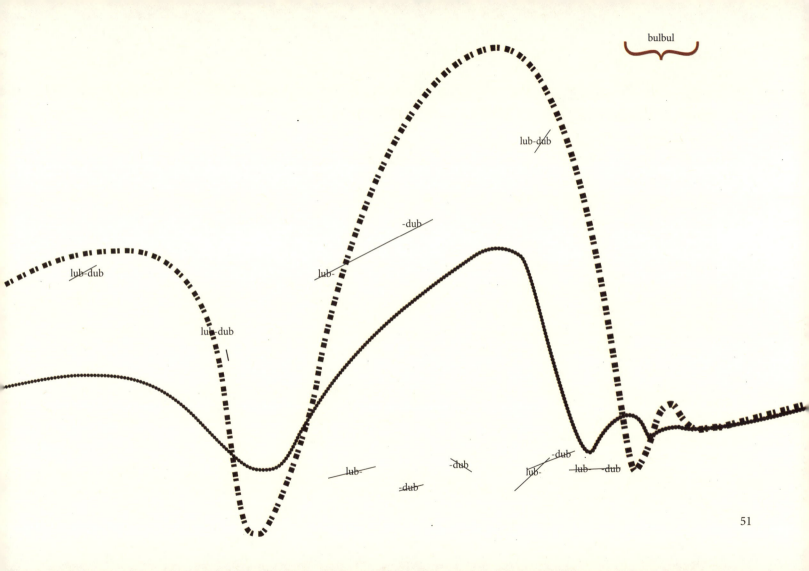

MUSE

breathless, the grouse leads us
steady as a rope through the trees. a marvel
to be undone or free or brown
or natural. to take up sound and space, or to deliberate the danger
of one's weight among the limbs
and free sparrows. she is here before us,
so close she almost seems to want
to be taken, and her body is beholden
to hunger that is not like our own—ours that comes
because we thought to come. she stays close enough
that we might be tempted to reach out suddenly,
the way the body just knows
when to gallop or swallow. and though she flies, she stays near enough
that we remark upon her face, let her sounds
be trapped within us in the places we keep
labyrinthine, watching her whip
off just when we might make of her smallness
an offering to ourselves. she hops and swoops
on a wound the wind makes
before it pools with the new air

of our laughter—we joke at how lazily
we could move and still hold her delicacy down
almost flat against the mossy ground. and though she cannot know
we have no interest in her children, in the children
of anyone—whether drowned or folded
like a veil—she knows we are animals that do not need
to need children to take them. she never lets us touch her.
we imagine she can be touched.

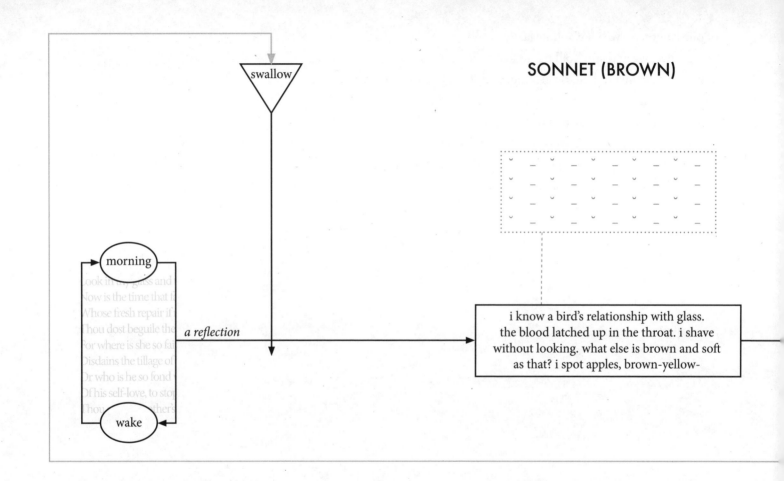

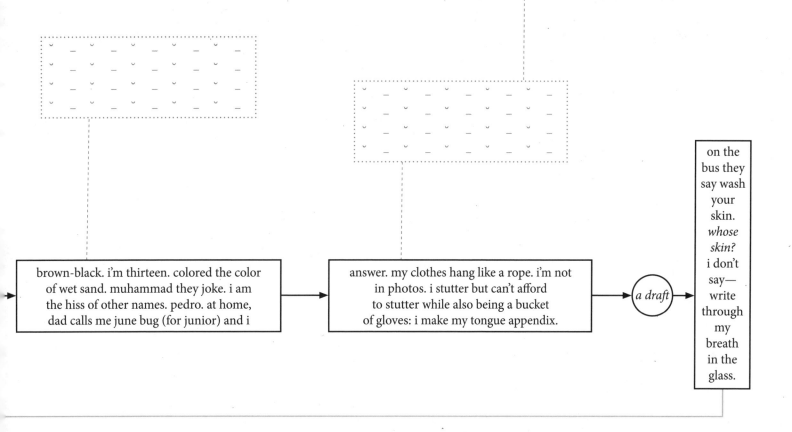

WHAT PHOENIX LEARNS IN PASSING

they say phoenix learns in passing.

what do i look like. really. how
is my sound. the ph in acid

and fool. flying's for the
slight and graceful birds or else

it's just buzzing. i make oatmeal

every morning, make like
pelicans and grieve. i am over

my body. they say i speak pigeon-

ish. one slur-
tongued man meant to be touching,

he said toucan. question mark. i overhear
all the time eight-legged

things (i am on the wall
unseen). jokes

mostly. great
if of my body!

imagine to have been reincarnated
colorless. in my youth

smiling like: yes of course
that's where i'm from.

out of fire, chicken whites

veal browns but what tans
the so-so tan of history. what do you call

a half-black? demiplague
but not the sun coming

up like a dolphin.
when you die and come back

how is that passing. call it a failure.
i am saying i'd be so happy to worm if i was

definitely a worm.

FEAR OF DOORS

i. my beef with karma is that if i deserve my misfortune—
the sneeze that unweaves a muscle in my back—then i might deserve

anything i have. even relief. ii. when i'm at the height
of my sadness i'm porous. when i'm fine

i am like an emperor penguin that knows the ice.
i say nothing but i know the color. iii. money is invented.

we should print more of it. iv. i disbelieve balance itself—let us tableflip the cosmos,
which cannot know the strange rates of exchange

between our bodies. v. calm often depends on the unheard
labor of others. a village to raise the flag of quiet up.

but one cry, even from a bird, unmakes it. vi. historically we've called it song. vii. on campus,
protestors chant to me: if butchers worked behind glass,

nobody would eat meat. viii. we used to have our fingers
in everything. ix. i cleaned the bone

saws and the cleavers, i knelt below the conveyers and sprayed the hose
until the roseate became clear: the butchers joke, leave fingerprints

on their gummy candy, their starbursts
and sour worms. only sometimes would they wash their hands.

x. though a building looks nothing like a pair of eyes,
they both bring the same fear in me. of flailing

as if flying is a possibility just out of reach. xi. something else i can't reconcile:
nothing is so astonishing as a moth. i mean it.

where they land, they leave silver. if one lights
upon your finger or your neck, they are costume jewelry.

in their place, or in their leaving. xii. i can feel this and be
afraid of them too. they clap like hands

devoid of bodies. xiii. i have a fear
of losing some visible part of me.

i saw once, in a movie, a man lose a finger
to a slammed door. xiv. i hate to kill them.

xv. i close. i open.
i wipe the silver from my hands.

LEGEND*

! imagine, from the inside, all the kind relentless reminders: *the outside of the house is brown. the outside of the house is brown*

@ as above, but this time be alien, disembodied & in space

glance at the memorial of your hands, & often, you'll see another person's hands, or someone says your name & you miss a beat. you say *oh did you mean me* & they say *no.* someone else's name

$ the off-white country of your mouth. fair-weather windows. an old chicago building (by way of the great migration). teeth that are each of them a door, that, once opened, will never close

% proof: *"If you put a spoonful of wine in a barrel full of sewage, you get sewage. If you put a spoonful of sewage in a barrel full of wine, you get sewage."*

^ here be dragons

& the holiest back alley of the eye,
behind even the spot
you've only ever thought of once.
the place in the grass where maybe nothing

* a key is a legend. both protect property

GERRYMANDER FOR A BLACK SENTENCE

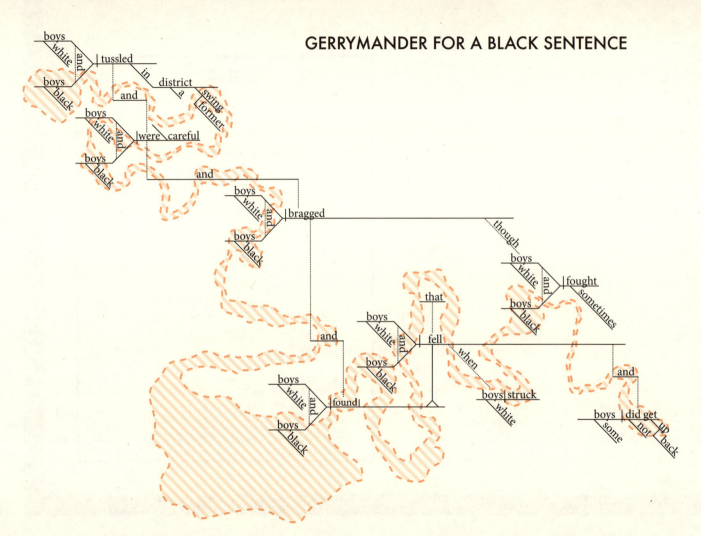

64

APOTHEOSIS

a brief history of kneeling

2015   new england patriot tom brady is seen with a maga cap in his locker. he refuses to explain—in football this is called a genuflect offense.

2016   colin kaepernick begins kneeling. it is his latest act of protest against police brutality. it is only performed during the national anthem.

2017   viewers are brought to their knees in a 3rd quarter comeback—the patriots win super bowl LI, just months after trump surprises even himself.

2018   in what's almost certainly a response to bombastic tweets made by president trump,

the NFL enacts a policy to fine players for kneeling.

2019   trump's knee-jerk reaction to covid is not to ready the nation for the disease but to ready the economy for it.

2020   the senate refuses to go forward

with convicting trump of anything.

2021   biden signs a bill honoring juneteenth. go forth and vote,

he says to those who know what juneteenth is.

2022   on trial for photographing kobe bryant's remains—photos that were then shared with a bartender and other civilians—deputy douglas johnson moves that new video footage be taken off the table, stating that the video is unrelated to the case at all.

the video in question is security footage of officer johnson kneeling

on the neck of inmate enzo escalante's head for 3 minutes.

concerning the trial at hand: the prosecution asks johnson

if he would do anything differently if he could.

"no sir" the records show.

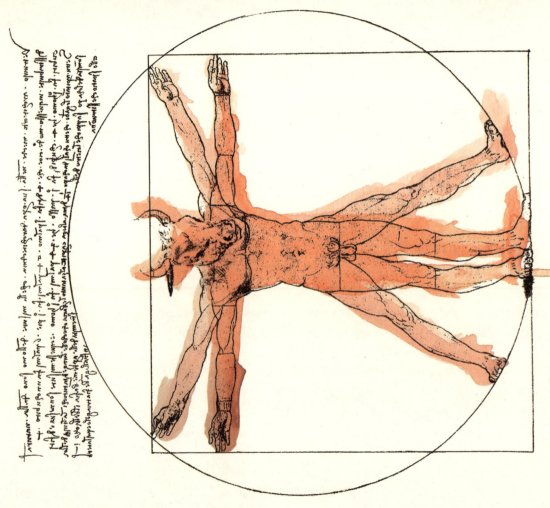

A TRANSLATION

Vitruvius, the architect, says in his work on architecture that the measurements of the human body are distributed by Nature. Bentham says even potential (that is, imagined) light can make a man. All that Ovid has to say about the Minotaur is this—he was a disgrace to his father's name. Is a man more like a building, a flower, or a shame? How is he measured if not, in all these cases, by cells?

The length of a man's outspread arms is equal to his cage From the roots of the hair to the bottom of the face is a tenth of a man's height; say hi, hello world from the tippy-top of the many-chambered heart; from the bottom of the chinny chin chin to the top of his head, one eighth; past the mirror past the wall, Minotaur sees the trees, how tall are they in stories; eighteen; it is hard to keep a man whole / whole man in a cage; from the top of the breast to the first crop of hair will be the seventh part of him; wonder & tongue; the beginning of the genitals marking the middle of a whole man; a subdivision, to be or not to be; from the bottom of the chin to the nose & from the roots of the hair to the eyebrows; broken mockingbirds trade in for a ring, rest now don't peep—the ear, a third of the face, an apartment window or a tree; what good is reasoning; what good is faith; put it to sleep, fool body, put it to sleep—leap!

67

SELF-PORTRAIT AS A BIRD THROUGH GLASS

I love how you never find their bodies, how they never rest their eyes. I love how their breasts are comforters unfolding by their breath. I love that pigeons live in the city, that underestimation never stopped a pigeon from unlatching itself or being old. I want them all unspooling in the air, and bridges that are half sigh and half pigeon. I want to harbor their coo and utilize it for energy. I want to learn to use them the way they want to be used. I want to pigeontail into a quiet night, to let their oddness sit in our thank god, some day, for the surprise. hands. You can never my fat who cares against my fat, know a language until you and finally nothing to worry quiet your own. I want people to write about them. to say. sunlight. Their leaving ships for land, or standing on their silence, now i am the wideness own on a marble stat- of my bed. they better never shave my face. ue in the though who is there to impress. mer of a field. I want to talk the fledgling dead? i'll be five again about the term "rock dove," argue with no specific reason. over whether or not it's imperialist. I want the media to implicate us in the pigeon problem, for a couple to sit with their asparagus and kids and realize none of this is far from them, whatever we think. I want oils and watercolors and inks. I want still life with pigeons, since not a one has ever been portrayed with soul: a flight of them around old bread. And how they're all the same. How all the world is here with them in hate, since they are rats adorned with angel wings, and the children down the street are free to chase their drag; they want to see a pigeon's rouge entirely. Let the pigeon have her pigment. Consider the pigeon's brown and green and everything, the brandishing of his nakedness to the sun, as if nothing is absolute—I love the pigeon's shoulders, tongues, and wedding nights. I love the pigeon's place in history, their obsession with living in the letters of our signs. I love their minds, or what I've come to believe is their theology. Who knows? Let the pigeons speak. Ask the closest pigeon for his number, for her middle name, if they are ready to die, if the sky gets crowded enough to consider war, if their stores are closed on Sundays. I want to be ready for them to be just like us, but more ready for them to be completely different. I don't want to waste any time tracing a pigeon's god to Abraham. I want to get started. Some of us feed pigeons. I love, sometimes, our care. I love, I think, the park bench. I love apples but I do not love pears. The weather. I love the pigeons, the revolution of wheel to sky. I love the newspaper greying in a different air.

CAPTION

your body (left) was 80 degrees / facing east / alas /—whose driveway was it?—or was it the stairs? // my temper / the crack of snow / peas // or else // in the summer // heated / light sashayed through gasoline / the belt buckle in a closed-off car // you are / angry like the sound a shutter makes / startling a squirrel under a tree // our fathers made us— / upset / never talk about work / money / love // i say i understand / i say i do because saying i don't was disastrous // what also didn't work was saying nothing // anyway i am too much like mine // like this // there's nothing here for me you say and i am too angry to admit anything // which means chicago // we are looking out the windows at what is now our world / a wall of bricks // the only titan i understand / is atlas / or what i mean is i can get that kind of pain // the kind that redefines // the shoulders // we've been arguing so long it turns into a regular conversation // the lady called it a new york view // that summer / the tires in a race / outside / the limits of god // sticking to the roads / never letting go except in big black pieces / a man yelled a slur at me and you didn't listen / i thought that was the barometer for love / or maybe it was kentucky / no i know it was / i remember it burst like a great beetle / a russet-colored fence / a slick green bottle / soda / was it / the ice cream man—remember him?—sheathing a cuss // when does the power to not say something become the cowardice of it // or after the fact // i said how was your day and i was glad / you did not ask back / you said fine / i said it too / blue-/ the sign over the market / children playing / red / rover / black-//ened toast // a depression in the skin left by the belt / you said i always made the eggs perfect / i felt it as a pressure i could hardly live up to // god (right) / you must be baffled // by endings // but i am not / i think of this a lot / whether you were ever really there / i snap / what do you expect me to do / now / i see you everywhere // here / the grass brown beyond return // you gave your word / your patience / yellow / dust / the blasted color of bricks / you gave me poetry // you gave me space / you only asked that i have faith / i had it / why else would i be here now (black star)

BLUEPRINT FOR A PRISON DEATH BED

the moral force between

any two people is still gravity

L the accused

the president *P*

Q

the right to refuse

R

silence

M *K*

mortar for the tower

N

O

juror *F*
juror *t*
juror *E*
juror juror *s*
juror juror *D*
juror *r*
juror *C*
juror *q*
juror *B*
juror *p*
A

THE GAMBLER

daedalus, presumably, lived.

less than a mile out from the slot in the water,
he thought: what am i to make

from this? his boy had been fearful
of shadows. daedalus doused every wick
in the house, had said what good is the light
if really there are monsters? it might've worked

if he were raising himself. you couldn't
just let him stay up? his wife had asked.

an irony in that, but not a lesson.
he was a man accustomed to work,
to fabricating, from the barest air, dignity, machines,
and equations. another time,

daedalus had left him
a bucket of wood. he assumed the worst that could come
from an engineer's son

would be fashioning some sentimental figure,
his father or a dove.

but the boy never touched it. the curse of labor

is that if you dream, your children sleep.
his hands knew the level and the awl. his boy knew water
stains on varnished wood.

that evening, he didn't command
the boy not to cry. softening in the fading light,
he bargained with him, instead:

don't you want to be a man?

he recalled his son's wet face slivered
by the dark, turning over. he never cried out,

from face to wings to face again.
like a quarter. daedelus, on the other hand,

spent, and far along the beach as if getting
to work. past the birds
who inherited their flight
and therefore made nothing
of it. but he made nothing

of it too. finally he found his hands
were holding the wings. both of them, somehow. at rest,
in his hands in the water.

SUBJUNCTIVE EMMETT TILL

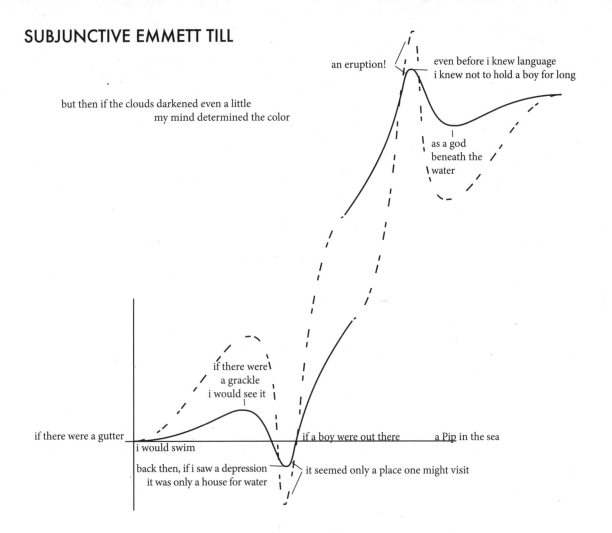

TENSES

after Annette Wong

	Simple	**Continuous**	**Perfect**
Present	listen good pigeon we live and **die**	true as winter come spring we **are dying**	we **have died** dove
Past	like this extending our arms out pretending the language of heaven is southern by way of the sky how we threw our voices our hands our backs remember heaving remember how we **died** to make stones ricochet	on and then into the lake and the city had plans that did not take into account any childhood how it put up the yellow tape and **was dying** to hem over the unassuming blue body	and hawk alike flower sellers commemorating the dying with the dead there was no quiet place remember brother that summer we thought we **had died** and went to heaven the sky black and white and black and white the old tradition
Future	body to body until the grave rebels spread a breathless anthem america i say if we **will die** someday so be it so be it to reimagine the world fair leave it to the young we want our children to be	to be just like us to hunger and play as we have always hungered and played even knowing our children our unaccounted-for promises **will be dying** ripening in the chicago sun times	never changing each riotous burst of light has always clarified what remains of our youth from those who **will have died** with us here stand and look up to us we've always been freest together our arms like gusts of wind that when we are tired flag and when we are most animated lift up cotton and bits of flame

THINGS I'VE FOUND LEFT IN THIS FIELD

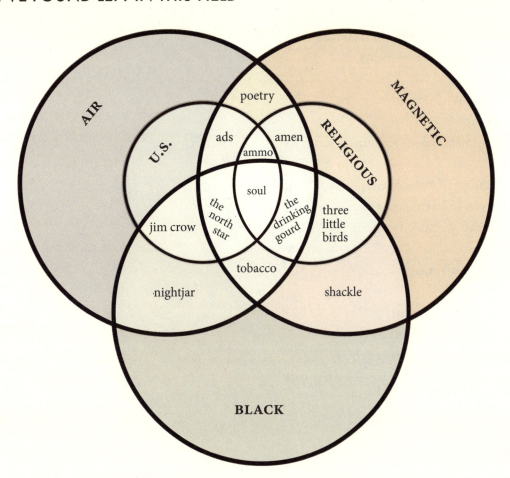

WALMART

we don't care because we're young. or if you ask me
i'll say i know the meaning of moments.

or any tragedy still has road to drive on (joy
is hourly) and so, so
what. so what if his nerves don't reconnect:

his grin in his retelling of the accident gives us that permission
        (and nerves—and endings—each of us imagines,
are more abstractions we can do without. breaks for water.

so much i know of it, of time,

i know from hoping for it to pass). so
we drink this or that when we feel it in our backs.
so he will favor new fingers, or learn a thing
i myself had already intended to learn as a party trick: to write

off-handed. you can be made half human
if you are paid to be half furnace,

                              your insides
hold heat the way a v8 does—the way a windowpane.

what happened: when he lifts the heavy case of orange pop
from the truck bed, his hand catches on the metal
frame of the conveyer and some of him spills across
the grey-black concrete. what's relief: that nothing shatters. we're split
apart. they promise to drive him, his open hand,

to the hospital as soon as he signs all the paperwork (they hold
the forms like film reels to keep them clean)

and on the line (which we are never to leave
except for the bathroom) the managers talk me through it,

here are the gloves, and the bleach, and the mop. i nod,
though how can they know like i know how inarticulate i am
with my intent? i have no plans. i say something that reads as a promise
and then, an upturned spider here against the window, brown, shaken slightly

by my breath, all the fingers closed as if this was the only way
a body knows to lie. i stand in the stall alone until i know it's done

UNDERGOD

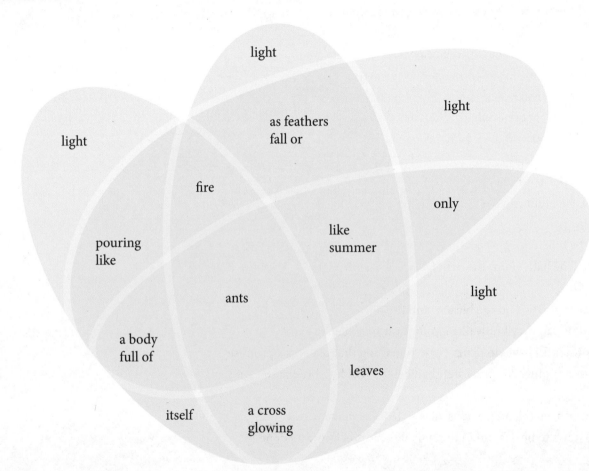

SEED

```
             gunmetal
                        ┐
                        ├── ash ──┐
             battleship ┘         │
                                  ├── black ──┐
             jet        ┐         │           │
                        ├── smoke ┘           │
             cadet      ┘                     │
                                              ├──────
             khaki      ┐                     │
                        ├── burnt umber ──┐   │
             umber      ┘                 │   │
                                          ├── brown ──┘
             bronze     ┐                 │
                        ├── dirt ─────────┘
             coffee     ┘
```

whitespace whitespace whitespace whitespace whitespace
whitespace whitespace whitespace whitespace white
whitespace whitespace whitespace whitespace wh
whitespace whitespace whitespace whitespace
whitespace whitespace whitespace whites
whitespace whitespace whitespace whi
whitespace whitespace whitespace
whitespace whitespace whitespa
whitespace whitespace whit
whitespace whitespace w
whitespace whitespac
whitespace whites
whitespace whit
whitespace white
whitespace whitesp
whitespace whitespac
whitespace whitespace w
whitespace whitespace wh
whitespace whitespace whit
whitespace whitespace whites
whitespace whitespace whitespa
whitespace whitespace whitespace
whitespace whitespace whitespace w

I can't deny that

my words   and again!
I maintain yet again they are for anyone
tended   if you'll excuse the expression   abundantly to seed
since they exist in space expressly for that purpose
           except   I should say   when they are reduced
in order to enjoy their sugar   a shame
to labor over
a thing that is already finished   all in order to have
God's bountiful and purple language   Consider that
in being shared   it encourages more sharing of it still
for my sake   forgive me   if I use God as a modifier   if i say
in this way
that language escapes me
every time
           can't you see my breath cannot help but white the air?

APOTHEOSIS

once upon a time, there was a boy
who struck another boy in the back of his head with a baseball bat
he did it without thinking, from a slow-moving car.

2015   new england patriot tom brady stares with a hand on his cheek. he enters an empty rhyme. this is called a genuflect offense.

2016   colin kaepernick begins kneeling, it is a late-stage protest against police brutality. it is plainly performed during the national anthem.

2017   viewers plunge bloody dollars in a bucket to watch things you super howdy'd. just months after trump surprises even himself.

2018   in what amounts to entirely the purpose, the bombastic tweets made by president trump,
and the bean bag as if they weigh the same.   the NFL enacts a policy to fine players for kneeling.

2019   any coward can hold a lighter in sure hatred. you hold them no less ready. the nation, he says, is that least of ready the economy for it.

2020   but am i saying that i understand? he meant it as a joke—the simple walking to goes toward

once i closed my eyes to see how long i could drive without thinking of anything.

2021   biden signs a bill honoring juneteenth go for to pay, wiping our hands on our pants
he says to those who know what juneteenth is the same way.

2022   on trial for photographing dead friends and shooting young men which were then shared with a bartender
and other civilians—deputy douglas johnson moves that the video footage be taken off the table,
stating that the video is unrelated to the case at all.   for an instant, i consider running after him

the video in question is security footage of officer johnson kneeling
on the neck of inmate enzo escalante's head for 3 minutes.
concerning the trial at hand: the prosecution asks johnson
if he would do anything differently if he could.

"no sir" the records show.

83

AP·PRE·HEN·SION

i'm young enough to have let the flowers slip my mind old enough to wilt to be a man i keep my tender under wraps as if it were good and natural a reagan quote can be seen gleaming from the owner's arm forearm i think this is it the rundown gas station predating me the store's air pregnant with a yellow evening light of my life i say nothing at first he can hear well damn love answer your phone hello can i help you understand this is a day for devotion and i am a fool a grave flower when held under scrutiny i walk as if i am not being watched and will soon enough return to you the suspect reception finally fails at the coolers and since i seem bound i take the lead i hold my hand all the way out thus our faces abstract in the black glass and our mouths cleave flush just us the light quiet my heart open at the register i see it red through the pane red the sound born red by the way the minute rose fell fire red

SERAPHIM

looking back i call the shapes we made
radical, an abstraction of birds—

because i cannot bear to just let them be.
maybe memories are not

to be tampered with, just as you do not touch
the venerable, the way

you do not hold an open wire (your name

spoken from myself to myself
to the sky). remembering is like the snow

i mean: even when i shouldn't be,

i am surprised. like seeing children in it, or squirrels
across a barren parking lot. really, testimony is beside the point:

like a tree that falls in the woods, there are, everywhere,
simple shapes of you

that make things happen—
even when i'm not there for them.

they go on, subatomically.
there's a propulsion to this feeling

of losing you: arm to snow to wing, the way age follows
forgetting being young. your color

and your voice too—light cannot move
a pendulum and yet it moves me. remember tethered motions

in the snow as if to fly. even in dreams,
the most essential quality of being

a bird has always been flight—
but this is an ideation of no bird really and is only

an obsession of the wingless: if a bird reasons with moonlight
the way i do with myself every night—

if it knows the air as holy—of the rapture of being carried,
coolly, to an underpass to escape the snow—

                                  i am saying if a bird sees as i can see
the rime-ensilvered window where i often stand alone—

if it sees things not only for what they are
but what they disclose—

surely then it cares for wings like i care for walking home,
and must know
as any being who has ever felt fire and ice

knows—as you and i know—what is life

and what is limbic. when a look
is merely expressionistic—what is feather

what is hinge and what is half-platonic form—
cast here in this place where once, together, we moved the snow.

AMERICAN LYRIC

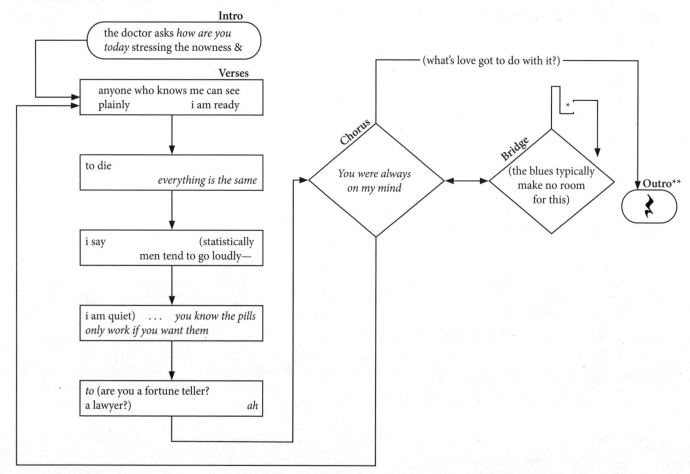

* *imagine, if you like, the Chi-Lites performance of "Oh Girl," the harp crying out at the end of the last "i don't know how"*
** *to be repeated until the sound is lost in the distance*

WAILING MAP

*At night [they would] march down
into the water singing as they marched...*

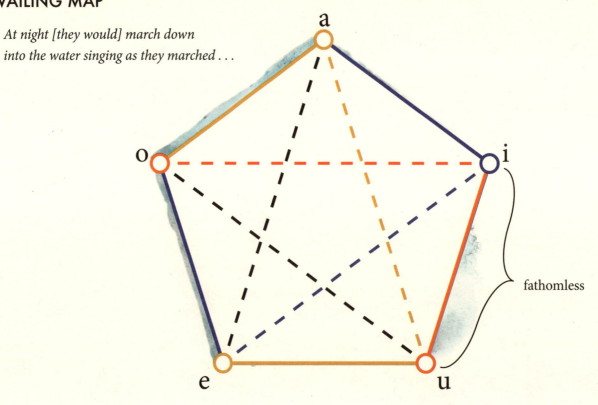

fathomless

*...the owners lost a number of them this way,
and finally had to stop the evening singing.*

—from John Spencer Bassett's *Slavery in the State of North Carolina*

LANDSCAPE WITH MONA LISA

about the surroundings: a grey and unknown wetted stone.

a scene that lies about
its height (too tall). it seems the kind
of place that makes wolves go gentle to the ankles
of their kings. some nameless bridge. fritillaria

imperialis. we can even make out in the hills
how the trees,

when made to stretch this way, become unseemly. longing
like this, overly,

is not imagistic but a feeling—a tendinitis. what a pain.
there's something remarkable about the face
that, since you hold it one way in your mind,

remains unreadable as a lark

(if that is the small, fast bird i saw once
going upward in a blur)

(i think that was the name. anthus? calcarius?) (i wrote it down
but i write everything down.)

(all i have are names and, regrettably, anything
to me could be a flower.)

UNCANNY COLUMBINE

*I cannot go on
restricting myself to images*

*because you think it is your right
to dispute my meaning.*

—LOUISE GLÜCK, "Clear Morning"

it's been some time since i considered suicide
at its first, i hardly thought of violence
but of being sorry, stepping back.

an apology pulls the pin
from the problem—
call it dappled light,
how certain flowers want to live

a columbine flowers easily
like this, after one
removes the dead.
i was subject. i observed.

violence calls from within,
discharges her passions upon false objects
montaigne said.

as if my center
or the train i would be trampled by
was either true or false

once we elided it by finding beautiful
the white center of something else.
but any smell long enough held becomes
nothing. now we do that.

SEED

the first name of air was water.
of love was mother, was never
clear, (but clear's was water).

the first name of winter was want, or
obsession (a matter perhaps
of inflection), and once, with my father,

i called death by his first name
which was stillness
(but stillness wakened). the first name

of miracle was ceremony. once, in desperation
i called her name and disappointment answered:
the first name of my uncle, mark,

was blood, and since it was the 90s
they had no medication. my first

name is father but i have no child (i am a junior),
and when he lived, since he lived,
i thought long about god, whose first name

i'd learned was absence. maybe in that way
of birds, who are make-believe except if you listen
closely or wish to sleep. i remember loving

to sing. i love it now, but not
like i remember. i sang with you, again
when he lived, when i learned the titles

but not a word of any song. i know my mother
can make herself cry remembering my name.
i know the first name of the grave was ground

and the ground somehow was heaven.

WE WERE MADE TO PLAY IN THE WHOLENESS OF THE FIELD

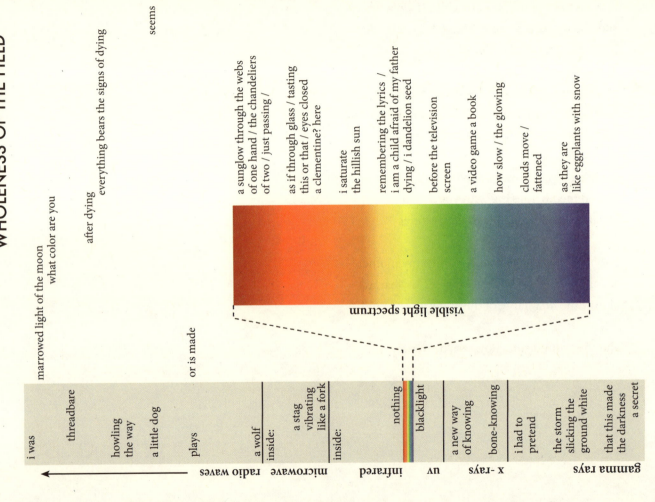

SOMETHING CAST FROM BRONZE

this is the black and white wilderness,
your body and all the birches
peeling, and rather than rest, you consider mastery.
then the breeze.
an orchestration of the outside
that steadies down your hand—the way
of sable to a painting of snow—or the bettering of your skin as it turns
directly in the sun, here above the tree line
where nothing hangs but the celestial—you feel how you'd ought to feel
    were you a single plate
inched utterly to the edge
of the world—here there is no time for thought—
and before the fall,
you imagine fighting—dragging all the other
    planets by their knees: the tea
    cups, or the coffee
(who, though, consumes? and who makes what is taken? and whose knees?).
not so far away, the forest burns.
the fence is a broken gate, the gate a sovereignty.
mocha, a lover once told you, is the beauty of your skin.

FIELD SWITCH

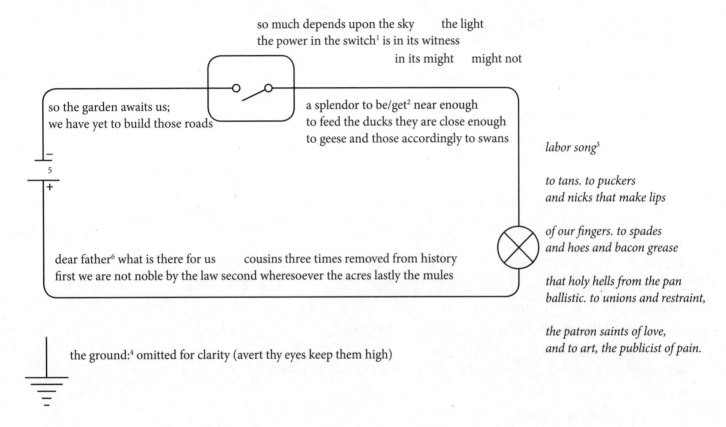

[1] see also: the willow trees
        (those your father ordered cut)

[2] elect snakes—
        name thy children ess
hear it in the yes
        ma'am yes sir every time you strike

[3] dash dash dash o
        dash dash dash god

[4] this is hell why the worldly at all

[5] why rest   wonder
        at any word that renders
        the distance between us a burden unworth
        the walk

[6] even the sun burns
            the midnight oil he wakes contused
      and speaking spry[1] his blacks in the first morning
          of their morning forced
              to meet his blues

WHO IS THERE TO EULOGIZE THE TREE

[1] a shadow extended long enough becomes just
the light

[2] you've never been tender. (moth wings. tobacco strung up to dry the color of men.) you can't walk to the car without stopping for your father to water the yard. he stares across it, bending over, thin as a country lost half to civil war (a cancer sign), the other half to ashes. he picks every weed as if they're his children—could be woven to a silken throne. you leave them be. whatever he believes, he believes. your whole theory of the sky would change if you crossed south of the equator. there, the north star evaporates. we play these games as children. killing games—who would you murder (or marry) if it meant meandering the stars close to home, keeping them from change? (you can try again to put hands to head to roots and stand, but every distant sun is diamond-set into the back of your father's father's land.) starshine and blood plays across the innocence (some vote ignorance) of trees. they say yours are your father's eyes. he says look at steve, who is army green and bends to the wind like a galaxy. sleeping every night beside him in the ward, your father didn't know your name. your dream is to be terrible (a monster or a worm) and ratchet back history and only after grossing be good. you're american. you could have said anything. you could have become anyone but of course you never did. your name unfurls from his name like onion skin. you've never seen your father cry. once, when his brother dies, you think you see it. he waters the snow at the place he poured the urn—your father's brother is a tree—or it's a trick of the light. fireworks. aurora borealis.

[3] a crow's memory is generational

[4] a distant kite

MIDSUMMER

frolic. set your leg against a tree as if to be
a branch. or failing that: relax—fold
the paper like this and say:
well, that's a very good question.
try to love your hands and let them be
their independent color. look, you say,
we have the same hair. the air all agog
with young laughter. listen, keith:
those are your nieces competing
with the earth. how easily
they make a trumpet of july. they are too brash
to hear the wolf call wilson. or
this is not the world that put the moon in you.
when you and your brother were younger
than money, you put your whole back
into pulling weeds to make room
for troughs and water, just to see
it run. now you never do. now your backwardness
settles in, as comfortable as your favorite
spoon. and you have a favorite spoon!

you used to invent new wounds,
and now you have the terror of rhyme.
and a colonial relationship with sleep—
what you can't make it do
you work around like a great stone
even weeds cannot undo. instead, you plant
the wicker of your back wherever it's green to see
what they see. to call it memory.

］
］ *youth*
］
］
］
］

—*Sappho*

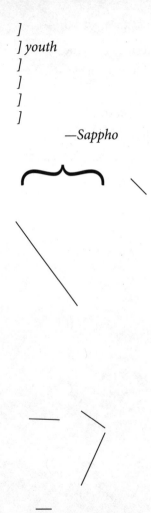

NOTES

Unless otherwise noted, all graphics were digitally created by the author.

A TRANSCENDENTAL FUNCTION

Non-algebraic; in mathematics, any equation that cannot be calculated solely by adding/subtracting, multiplying/dividing, or raising to a power/root extraction.

The pictured graph is a cosine ($\cos(x) = y$) and is an example of a transcendental function.

MEMORIAL

The full quote from the Associated Press article "Project aims to mark dozens of American slave trade ports":

> "We're just simply saying mark the place where it began,' said Ann Chinn, who founded the Middle Passage project. 'In the same way, people marked Plymouth, they marked Jamestown, they marked St. Augustine. Well, in each of those places, Africans were there too."

The Middle Passage Ceremonies and Port Markers Project was created in order to "place markers at 40 ports along the Atlantic and Gulf coasts where slaves arrived or where ships were sent to be used in the trade."

The Middle Passage refers to the second part of a three-part journey. 1) Starting in England, traders sailed to various locations in West Africa. 2) From there, ships embarked on the Middle Passage by taking enslaved Africans to America for sale. 3) Finally, ships set sail back to England.

Starting in the 16th century, the transatlantic slave trade forcibly moved and enslaved over 12 million Africans. This number does not include the hundreds of thousands (possibly millions) that died during the journey.

Occurring in 1967, *Loving v. Virgina* (388 U.S. 1) was a Supreme Court decision that ruled that laws banning interracial marriage were unconstitutional. The case was brought to court by Richard Loving (white) and Mildred Loving (Black), who had been sentenced to prison for violating Virginia's Racial Integrity Act by marrying.

THE INVITATION

Often misattributed to Aesop, "The Scorpion and the Frog" is a very young fable in the lifespan of fables. The first known appearance of it is in the Russian novel *The German Quarter* by Lev Nitoburg in 1933.

UNCANNY EMMETT TILL

Image created by author, based on the Wikimedia Commons image (shown here) created by user Smurrayinchester, which itself was based on the original image created by Masahiro Mori and Karl MacDorman.

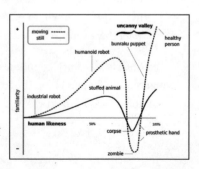

A philosophical concept first described by robotics professor Masahiro Mori and widely used in the fields of robotics and computer graphics, the uncanny valley concerns human representation.

It posits that people are most comfortable when they know for certain that something they are looking at is definitely not human, or when they have been fully convinced something that is *not* human *is* human.

Represented on the graph: on the far left are visuals easily identifiable as not human. On the far right are representations that look so human that we are "tricked" into believing we are looking at a true human (think: very well done computer graphics from a Marvel movie). The dip—the valley—are things that are not quite human enough.

Emmett Till (July 25, 1941–August 28, 1955) was a Black child who, in 1955, was accused by Carolyn Bryant of whistling at her in her family's grocery store. Bryant was 21 at the time; Till, 14.

Roy Bryant, Carolyn's husband, and his two brothers Leslie Milam and J. W. Milam, abducted Till. After three days, Till's body was found in the Tallahatchie River. Two Black publications, *Jet* magazine and *The Chicago Defender*, published photos of Till's mutilated body with the permission of his mother Mamie Till. She was quoted to have said: "Let the world see what I've seen."

Roy Bryant and J. W. Milam were acquitted by an all-white jury and, protected from re-prosecution by double jeopardy, admitted to the murder in a 1956 *Look* magazine interview.

In June of 2022, Till's family discovered a warrant addressed to Roy Bryant, J. W. Milam, and Carolyn Bryant that said the three "did willfully, unlawfully and feloniously and without lawful authority, forcibly seize and confine and kidnap" Emmett Till. While Roy Bryant and J. W. Milam had passed away (in 1994 and 1980 respectively), Carolyn Bryant was never prosecuted—the warrant notes that Bryant was never arrested because she could not be located. In August of 2022, a grand jury in Mississippi declined to indict Bryant, citing a lack of evidence. Less than a year later, Bryant died (April 25, 2023).

LINE DANCE FOR AN AMERICAN TEXTBOOK

In the *Quartz* article "America's wholesome square dancing tradition is a tool of white supremacy," Robyn Pennacchia writes that the tradition of teaching square dancing in gym class owes its roots to Henry Ford who heavily campaigned for schools to teach it. She writes: "By bringing back square dancing, as well as other primarily Anglo-Saxon dances like waltzes and quadrilles, Ford believed he would be able to counteract what he saw as the unwholesome influence of jazz on America." While jazz was invented by African Americans, Ford believed that it was invented by Jewish people seeking world domination, and spread this conspiracy through the publication of a four-volume set of antisemitic booklets entitled *The International Jew*.

VIRGIN AND CHILD IN MAJESTY SURROUNDED BY SIX ANGELS

Cimabue (Cenni di Pepo). Oil painting on panel, 280 x 427 cm. Painted in the Byzantine style. Located in the Louvre, Paris, France.

MELTING POT

As the National Museum of American History puts it, "'Melting Pot' is a term that was used to describe Americanization in which immigrants adopt American culture and abandon culture from their home country." However, this concept is seldom described in terms of loss—of a language, culture, or identity—but of abundance, creation, or production: the focus is not on the ingredients but the stew.

108

The metaphor of the melting pot was in use as far back as the 1780s.

The pie chart was invented by Scottish engineer and economist William Playfair and first appeared in the seminal *Statistical Breviary* in 1801. Though it is one of the most widely used statistical graphs in the world, data visualization professionals often recommend against its use because of the practical difficulty of comparing data within the chart.

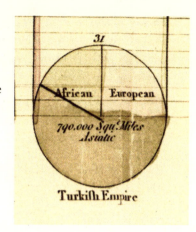

PROCESSING EMMETT TILL

While visually similar to a schematic created by Jamais Cascio in the article "The Second Uncanny Valley," this image is unrelated to it (making it a kind of visual or philosophical carcinization).

In mathematics, *reflection* is fairly difficult to define in layman's English despite the intuitive nature of the concept of reflection (even before mirrors, there was still water). This graph is reflective along the Y-axis, making it an example of bilateral symmetry, one of the most common (but not the only) kinds of reflection in nature.

SEVERAL DEFINITIONS OF "PLAY" IN WHICH I NEVER SAY THE WORD ONCE

Merriam-Webster lists 26 definitions of "play" as a noun and 62 definitions for "play" as a verb.

ANGLES OF INCIDENCE

In optics, a ray of light approaching a surface (such as a mirror) is called the incident ray. The ray of light bouncing from that mirror is called the reflected ray. The angle of these two rays are exactly equal—the angle of the original ray of light is called the angle of incidence.

The image (digital and gouache) appearing in the poem is based on one found in *The*

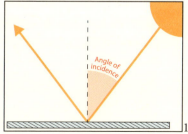

109

Foundations of Geometry by David Hilbert, courtesy of Project Gutenberg. Published in 1902, the book is a collection of lectures given from 1898–1899 that were meant to clarify the teachings of Greek mathematician Euclid (the "father of geometry"). The shapes approximate shapes and locations in Central Park, obtained via Google Maps.

TO THE GIRL(S) THAT DATED ME TO UNRAVEL THEIR WHITE FATHER

It wasn't until I was 28 that I dated someone whose parents were okay with my race.

TO THE WARMTH A BELLY MAKES WHEN SPARE AGAINST ANOTHER BELLY

Not that I asked.

SPELL TO TRACE A RAINBOW TO ITS APOGEE

A parabola is a curve formed by intersecting a circular cone and a plane—practically, the graph of a parabola looks like the trajectory of something launched from the ground, arcing through the air, and landing back on the ground.

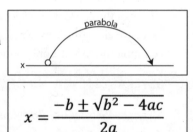

The quadratic formula was first discovered by Simon Stevin in 1594 and published in the form we know by René Descartes in 1637 in *La Géométrie*. The formula is used to solve for both the points (x) that cross the horizon. In the above example, the quadratic equation could be used to calculate where something began and where it ended.

Trayvon Martin was shot and killed by George Zimmerman on February 26, 2012. Zimmerman followed Martin, who was walking back from the convenience store to his father's fiancée's home in Miami Gardens, Florida. Zimmerman, who was part of the community watch and thought Martin looked suspicious, had called the police and been told not to pursue

Martin. At trial, Zimmerman claimed he felt threatened and had shot Martin in self-defense. He was acquitted of second-degree murder and manslaughter under Florida's "stand your ground" law, which grants citizens the ability to use deadly force when the victim is at risk of being killed or seriously injured. Martin was 17 years old at the time; Zimmerman, 28.

BATTER BREAD, MULATTO STYLE (1935)

The recipe is quoted in its entirety from *The Southern Cook Book of Fine Old Recipes*, compiled and edited by Lillie S. Lustig, S. Claire Sondheim, and Sarah Rensel and first published in 1935. The cookbook contains four instances of the word *mulatto* and four instances of the word *nigger*. The cookbook contains illustrations (pictured to the right) as well. Called "decorations," they are courtesy of H. Charles Kellum.

THERE'S A CONCEPT CALLED CHRONOSTASIS

Derived from Greek: *chronos* (time) + *stasis* (standing).

THE UNCANNY PUMP FAKE

In medicine, a healthy heart is described as making two distinct sounds when pumping blood. The first heart sound (S_1) is the *lub* and the second heart sound (S_2) is the *dub* in the *lub-dub* of a heart beating.

The folk story of flying Africans, told by African Americans starting from the time of slavery, held that some Africans were able to fly back to Africa. In some stories, Africans turned to birds, in some they flew without shape-shifting, and in others (like in the case of John the Conqueror) rode birds.

SONNET (BROWN)

A flow chart is a diagram outlining the steps or processes to complete a task. It was first introduced in a presentation at the American Society of Mechanical Engineers in 1921 by Frank and Lillian Gilbreth.

The concept of "stress" exists across languages, but in modern English it is so subtle that it is often difficult to decide what syllables of a sentence are or are not stressed. Stress is often described as the portion of a word that is most "emphasized"—the ABE in *unable*. In classical scansion (the study and documentation of stress and unstressed syllables in a poem), a stress is marked with an en dash and an unstressed syllable with a breve.

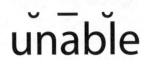

The contemporary sonnet in America follows very few consistent rules. Most commonly, it is 14 lines long, but it may or may not be metrical (following a strict pattern of stress vs. unstressed syllables), and may or may not rhyme.

WHAT PHOENIX LEARNS IN PASSING

In Greek mythology, a phoenix is born from the ashes (in some legends, the decomposed body) of a phoenix.

FEAR OF DOORS

Entamaphobia is the fear of doors.

LEGEND

Apocryphally attributed to German philosopher Arthur Schopenhauer, the quote "If you put a spoonful of wine in a barrel full of sewage, you get sewage. If you put a spoonful of sewage in a barrel full of wine, you get sewage," touches on common beliefs about goodness and purity.

In America, the one-drop rule is an example of hypodescent, the automatic assignment of children with mixed ancestry to the ethnic group of lower status. The legal principle was struck down by the Supreme Court in the *Loving v. Virginia* case of 1967.

GERRYMANDER FOR A BLACK SENTENCE

In linguistics, a sentence diagram is a graphical representation of the grammatical structures of a sentence.

Gerrymandering is the practice of drawing the boundaries of a voting block (often in absurd labyrinthine ways) in order to manipulate the power of that block of votes. The following image, created by Steve Nass and obtained from Wikimedia Commons, illustrates how the same number of votes can be used to favor either of two parties through gerrymandering.

A TRANSLATION

Digital (and watercolor) composite image of two scanned images.

1. *Vitruvian Man* (on following page), Leonardo da Vinci (1490). Pen and ink drawing, 34.4 cm × 24.5 cm, Gallerie dell'Accademia, Venice.

2. *Recto: An Ox*, Leonardo da Vinci (c. 1517–20). Red chalk on paper, 12.4 cm. × 17.7 cm, Royal Collection Trust, United Kingdom.

The *Vitruvian Man* is a drawing portraying da Vinci's idea of an ideally proportioned man. His measurements are modifications based on ones made by Vitruvius, a 1st century BC Roman architect, in the third volume of his book *Ten Books on Architecture*. The writing of the second page are da Vinci's notes on proportions. Ex: "From below the chin to the top of the head is one-eighth of the height of the man."

In Greek myth, Poseidon, god of the sea, gave Minos, king of the island of Crete, a white bull to sacrifice. When Minos refused to sacrifice it, Poseidon cursed Minos's wife, Pasiphaë to lust for the Cretan Bull. Pasiphaë asked Daedalus, a gifted inventor and architect, to build a wooden cow for her to hide within, allowing her to mate with the bull. Her son, Asterion (or "starry one") is better known as the Minotaur ("bull of Minos").

SELF-PORTRAIT AS A BIRD THROUGH GLASS

With text from "I Find Myself Defending Pigeons," Wilson, Keith S. *Fieldnotes on Ordinary Love*. Copper Canyon Press, 2019.

BLUEPRINT FOR A PRISON DEATH BED

Image from the math textbook *An Elementary Treatise on Solid Geometry* by Charles Smith, first published in 1884 and courtesy of the HathiTrust Digital Library.

As reported in Clint Smith's *How the Word is Passed*, when Louisiana transitioned from executions by electric chair to lethal injection in 1991, inmates were instructed to build the prison death bed. They refused.

The concept of the panopticon was theorized by philosopher Jeremy Bentham. The idea can be summarized by the following scenario: a tower exists at the center of a prison. Prisoners cannot see into the tower but the tower is capable of seeing into any cell at any time. A prisoner cannot know if he is being watched, and according to Bentham, the idea that he *might* be being watched at any time will mean that he always behaves *as if* he is being watched.

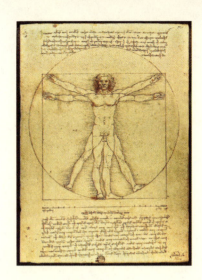

THE GAMBLER

In Greek myth, Minos, the king of Crete, ashamed and afraid of his stepson, the Minotaur, intended to imprison him. He ordered the architect Daedalus to build a labyrinth. This labyrinth was so complicated that Daedalus and his son Icarus were unable to find their way back. Daedalus built wings of wax for them both to fly to safety, warning Icarus not to fly too close to the sun for fear of the wax melting.

SUBJUNCTIVE EMMETT TILL

In grammar, a mood is a category of verb that expresses the speaker's view of reality. The subjunctive mood, for instance, is used to express things imagined or hoped. One way to identify something written in the subjunctive mood is the use of "were," for instance, "If I were happier, I would wake up earlier in the morning."

TENSES

Verbs that are conjugated in simple tense indicate things that are factual. Continuous tense indicates events that are in the act of happening. Perfect tense describes events that have already happened.

THINGS I'VE FOUND LEFT IN THIS FIELD

The Venn diagram, popularized by mathematician and philosopher John Venn in his 1881 book *Symbolic Logic*, are diagrams that show the relations between sets of information. Items are placed according to their relation to the categories indicated by the circles—when circles overlap, items within that overlap share commonalities with both circles.

SEED

A "bracket" is a kind of tree diagram used to determine and/or keep track of competitions. "Seeding," in this practice, is the act of estimating the best (or favored) teams/players ahead of time to ensure an interesting competition.

BONUS ACTIVITY

Whether or not a literary work survives its author is not only a matter of "quality" but also of platform. Shakepeare's increased popularity in the 18th century cannot be separated from the radical increase of spoken English during the height of British imperialism. Or, an author's work might be revived after falling into relative obscurity as Alice Walker revived Zora Neale Hurston's work when she wrote "In Search of Zora Neale Hurston" for *Ms.* magazine.

William Carlos Williams's 1934 poem "This Is Just to Say" has never *not* appeared in any of the six editions of the *Norton Anthology of Poetry*. Norton anthologies of literature and poetry are often the only assigned book used in classes teaching those subjects.

Even when "This Is Just to Say" is absent from an anthology, as it was in the *Penguin Anthology of 20th Century Poetry* (edited by Rita Dove), it is practically unthinkable not to include other poems by Williams—some amount of pages is nearly always devoted to him (or to one of a short list of other poets). To challenge the canon by devoting fewer pages to a poet like Williams in favor of some other poet is always a recipe for pushback, as when, in response to the Penguin anthology, Helen Vendler wrote an article for *The New York Review* entitled "Are These the Poems to Remember?": "Of the twenty poets born between 1954 and 1971 (closing the anthology), fifteen are from minority communities (Hispanic, Black, Native American, or Asian American), and five are white (two men, three women). Dove's tipping of the balance obeys a populist aesthetic voiced in the introduction."

Dove's response to the many accusations asserted in that article, also published in *The New York Review*, includes the following: "The amount of vitriol in Helen Vendler's review betrays an agenda beyond aesthetics."

AP·PRE·HEN·SION

homophones: words that sound the same but are spelled differently. Ex: *so* vs. *sew*.

homographs: words that are written the same but have different pronunciations. Ex: *I wind up the clock* vs. *the wind blew the leaves*.

homonyms: words that are spelled and pronounced the same but are different words. Ex: *he is a bright student* vs. *that is a bright light*.

Appropriately going by many names, a "crash blossom" is a sentence (usually a headline) with (usually temporary) ambiguous meaning. The term was coined by editor Mike O'Connell and is based on a *Japan Today* headline: "Violinist Linked to JAL Crash Blossoms." In this case, the crash is not what blossoms, but the violinist linked to a previous JAL crash is what blossoms.

AMERICAN LYRIC

This diagram is a flow chart (see: "sonnet (brown)").

The symbol in the "outro" panel is a quarter rest, from musical notation.

"Composer Gustav Holst understood the power of the fade-out and employed one of the first at a 1918 concert. For the "Neptune" section of *The Planets*, Holst had the women's choir sing in a room offstage. Toward the end, he instructed, the door should be closed very slowly: 'This bar is to be repeated until the sound is lost in the distance.' Given the subject matter—Neptune was thought to be the most distant planet in the solar system—Holst's attempt to conjure the remoteness of the planet and the mysteries of the cosmos makes sense." From "A Little Bit Softer Now, a Little Bit Softer Now" by William Weir for *Slate*.

WAILING MAP

Watercolor and digital composite.

Scholars debate as to the source of the legend of the flying African (See: "the uncanny pump fake"). One theory concerns the events of Igbo Landing, a mass suicide by drowning by African slaves. Accounts differ, but in May of 1803, the slave ship *York* met with rebellion by around 75 enslaved Igbo people (captured from what is now Nigeria). Those slaves drowned their captors and grounded in Dunbar Creek on St. Simons Island in Georgia. Some subset of the remaining slaves were said to have drowned themselves. Scholars theorize that oral traditions explained those missing Igbo people as having walked back over the water, or flown, to Africa.

LANDSCAPE WITH MONA LISA

Seen on right: Leonardo da Vinci. Oil on poplar panel. 77 x 53 cm. Located in the Louvre, Paris, France.

UNCANNY COLUMBINE

In computer graphics, transformations are equations done in order to modify and/or move graphics (often for animations). A rotation (or radial transformation) is one example of this.

WE WERE MADE TO PLAY IN THE WHOLENESS OF THE FIELD

Image (digital) based on a Wikipedia image for the article "Electromagnetic spectrum," created by user Penubag.

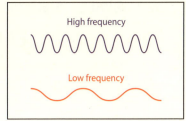

An electromagnetic wave's frequency determines what we call it, as well as how we physically interact with it. Waves with very high frequencies are highly destructive to matter—a gamma ray (with a frequency of 300 EHz) is able to move through lead and can destroy organic material, including DNA. Light, on the other hand, has a much lower frequency, and our eyes are designed to see it. The length of a wave determines the color we perceive. For example, if the wavelength of an electromagnetic wave is 400 nm, we see it as purple; if it is 700 nm, we see it as red.

FIELD SWITCH

A schematic circuit diagram represents the parts and connections of an electric circuit, allowing someone to re-create that electronic component.

The image portrays a simple light circuit. The battery supplies power. The switch, when toggled, closes the circuit and turns on the light. The bottom of the diagram is a shorthand reminder to include a "ground." In electronics, a ground is a safety measure—it is a direct connection to the earth that functions as an additional path for electricity to travel in the case of a short circuit.

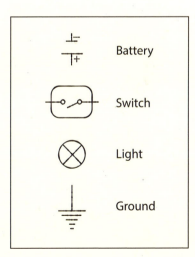

WHO IS THERE TO EULOGIZE THE TREE

"The first footnote drifts somewhere in a universe of manuscripts and books, eluding our discovery the way the original bright star of the skies eludes astronomers." From *The Footnote: A Curious History* by Anthony Grafton.

{

Epigraph from Sappho, fragment 87D. Translated by Anne Carson in *If Not, Winter: Fragments of Sappho*.

SOURCES

A TRANSCENDENTAL FUNCTION

Britannica, "Transcendental Function," last updated April 15, 2011, https://www.britannica.com/science/transcendental-function.

THE INVITATION

Wikipedia, "The Scorpion and the Frog," last updated December 14, 2024, https://en.wikipedia.org/wiki/The_Scorpion_and_the_Frog.

UNCANNY EMMETT TILL

Wikipedia, "Uncanny Valley," last updated January 21, 2025, https://en.wikipedia.org/wiki/Uncanny_valley.

Rina Diane Caballar, "What Is the Uncanny Valley?," *IEEE Spectrum*, November 6, 2019, https://spectrum.ieee.org/what-is-the-uncanny-valley.

Wright Thompson, "His Name Was Emmett Till," *The Atlantic*, September 2021, https://www.theatlantic.com/magazine/archive/2021/09/barn-emmett-till-murder/619493/.

Chuck Johnston, "Grand Jury Declines to Indict Carolyn Bryant Donham, the Woman Whose Accusations Led to the Murder of Emmett Till," CNN, last updated August 10, 2022, https://www.cnn.com/2022/08/09/us/emmett-till-carolyn-bryant-no-indictment-reaj/index.html.

LINE DANCE FOR AN AMERICAN TEXTBOOK

Robyn Pennacchia, "America's Wholesome Square Dancing Tradition Is a Tool of White Supremacy," *Quartz*, December 17, 2017, https://qz.com/1153516/americas-wholesome-square-dancing-tradition-is-a-tool-of-white-supremacy.

VIRGIN AND CHILD IN MAJESTY SURROUNDED BY SIX ANGELS

Cimabue, *The Virgin and Child in Majesty Surrounded by Six Angels*, c. 1270, oil on panel, 280 × 427 cm, Louvre, Paris, https://www.wikiart.org/en/cimabue/the-virgin-and-child-in-majesty-surrounded-by-six-angels.

BrdLvr!312, "Too Many Religious Paintings for Me," review of Louvre Museum, Paris, March 16, 2016, Tripadvisor, https://www.tripadvisor.com/ShowUserReviews-g187147-d188757-r356035452-Louvre_Museum-Paris_Ile_de_France.html.

MELTING POT

United Auto Workers, *The Melting Pot*, 1962, poster, 22 in × 19 in (55.88 cm × 48.26 cm), Detroit, Michigan, ref. no. 1988.0701.11, https://americanhistory.si.edu/collections/search/object/nmah_1050823.

Wikipedia, "*The Melting Pot* (play)," last updated August 6, 2024, https://en.wikipedia.org/wiki/The_Melting_Pot_(play).

Wiki 2, "File:Playfair-piechart.jpg," February 2, 2007, https://wiki2.org/en/File:Playfair-piechart_jpg.

Wikipedia, "William Playfair," last updated January 25, 2025, https://en.wikipedia.org/wiki/William_Playfair.

Steve Fenton, "Pie Charts Are Bad," Steve Fenton website, last updated October 21, 2022, https://www.stevefenton.co.uk/blog/2009/04/pie-charts-are-bad/.

PROCESSING EMMETT TILL

Wikipedia, "Symmetry in Mathematics," last updated January 5, 2025, https://en.wikipedia.org/wiki/Symmetry_in_mathematics.

Jamais Cascio, "The Second Uncanny Valley," Open the Future website, October 27, 2007, http://www.openthefuture.com/2007/10/the_second_uncanny_valley.html.

SEVERAL DEFINITIONS OF "PLAY" IN WHICH I NEVER SAY THE WORD ONCE

Merriam-Webster Dictionary, "play," accessed January 23, 2025, https://www.merriam-webster.com/dictionary/play.

ANGLES OF INCIDENCE

Mr Riddz Science, "What Is the Angle of Incidence?," posted January 18, 2015, https://www.youtube.com/watch?v=M95GQgPsomE&ab.

Wikipedia, "Central Park Jogger Case," January 22, 2025, https://en.wikipedia.org/wiki/Central_Park_jogger_case.

"*The Foundations of Geometry*, David Hilbert" listing, Goodreads, accessed January 24, 2025, https://www.goodreads.com/book/show/1635912.The_Foundations_of_Geometry.

SPELL TO TRACE A RAINBOW TO ITS APOGEE

Wikipedia, "Quadratic Formula," last updated January 2, 2025, https://en.wikipedia.org/wiki/Quadratic_formula.

Wikipedia, "Trayvon Martin," last updated November 17, 2024, https://en.wikipedia.org/wiki/Trayvon_Martin.

BATTER BREAD, MULATTO STYLE (1935)

Lillie S. Lustig, *Southern Cook Book* (Applewood, 2007).

THE UNCANNY PUMP FAKE

Wikipedia, "Heart Sounds," last updated February 12, 2024, https://en.m.wikipedia.org/wiki/Heart_sounds.

Jason R. Young, "All God's Children Had Wings," *Journal of Africana Religions*, vol. 5, no. 1 (Penn State University, 2017), 50–70, https://www.jstor.org/stable/10.5325/jafrireli.5.1.0050.

Samuel Momodu, "Igbo Landing Mass Suicide (1803)," BlackPast, October 25, 2016, https://www.blackpast.org/african-american-history/events-african-american-history/igbo-landing-mass-suicide-1803/.

Thomas Hallock, "How a Mass Suicide by Slaves Caused the Legend of the Flying African to Take Off," The Conversation, February 18, 2021, https://theconversation.com/how-a-mass-suicide-by-slaves-caused-the-legend-of-the-flying-african-to-take-off-153422.

SONNET (BROWN)

Matthew Jones, "English Intonation: Stressed and Unstressed Syllables," Magoosh IELTS Blog, May 18, 2021, https://magoosh.com/ielts/english-intonation-stressed-and-unstressed-syllables.

Wikipedia, "Flowchart," last updated, November 19, 2024, https://en.wikipedia.org/wiki/Flowchart.

Poetry Foundation, "Sonnet," Glossary of Poetic Terms, https://www.poetryfoundation.org/education/glossary/sonnet.

WHAT PHOENIX LEARNS IN PASSING

Wikipedia, "Phoenix (mythology)," last updated January 18, 2025, https://en.wikipedia.org/wiki/Phoenix_(mythology).

FEAR OF DOORS

"Fear of Doors Phobia—Entamaphobia," FEAROF, accessed January 23, 2025, https://www.fearof.net/fear-of-doors-phobia-entamaphobia/.

GERRYMANDER FOR A BLACK SENTENCE

Wikimedia Commons, "File:How to Steal an Election—Gerrymandering.svg," February 22, 2015, https://commons.wikimedia.org/wiki/File:How_to_Steal_an_Election_-_Gerrymandering.svg.

A TRANSLATION

Joannes Jonstonus, *Taurus Castratus Bos; Verschnittener Ochs.*, 1655, print of engraving, New York Public Library Digital Collection, ref. no. b15398144.

Leonardo da Vinci, *Recto: An Ox*, c. 1517–20, red chalk on paper, 12.4 cm × 17.7 cm, RCIN 912364, Royal Collection Trust, United Kingdom, https://www.rct.uk/collection/912364/recto-an-ox-verso-a-donkey.

Leonardo da Vinci, *Vitruvian Man*, c. 1590, pen on paper, 13.6 in × 10 in (34.6 cm × 25.5 cm), Galleria Nazionale di Parma, https://en.wikipedia.org/wiki/Vitruvian_Man.

BLUEPRINT FOR A PRISON DEATH BED

Clint Smith, *How the Word Is Passed: A Reckoning with the History of Slavery Across America* (Little, Brown, 2021).

Charles Smith, *An Elementary Treatise on Solid Geometry* (Macmillan, 1920), https://archive.org/details/elementarytreati00smituoft/page/n5/mode/2up.

The Ethics Centre, "Ethics Explainer: The Panopticon," Ethics.org, July 18, 2017, https://ethics.org.au/ethics-explainer-panopticon-what-is-the-panopticon-effect.

THE GAMBLER

Wikipedia, "Daedalus," last updated January 17, 2025, https://en.wikipedia.org/wiki/Daedalus.

Wikipedia, "Pasiphaë," last updated January 3, 2025, https://en.wikipedia.org/wiki/Pasipha.

THINGS I'VE FOUND LEFT IN THIS FIELD

Wikipedia, "John Venn," last updated November 27, 2024, https://en.wikipedia.org/wiki/John_Venn.

Will Kenton, "What Is a Venn Diagram? Meaning, Examples, and Uses," Investopedia, July 29, 2024, https://www.investopedia.com/terms/v/venn-diagram.asp.

SEED

Wikipedia, "Bracket (tournament)," last updated January 19, 2025, https://en.wikipedia.org/wiki/Bracket_(tournament).

BONUS ACTIVITY

Kyle Bachan, "Still Searching Out Zora Neale Hurston," *Ms.*, February 2, 2011, https://msmagazine.com/2011/02/02/still-searching-out-zora-neale-hurston/.

Alice Walker, "In Search of Zora Neale Hurston," *Ms.*, March 1975, 74–89, https://www.allisonbolah.com/site_resources/reading_list/Walker_In_Search_of_Zora.pdf.

Helen Vendler, "Are These the Poems to Remember?," review of *The Penguin Anthology of Twentieth-Century American Poetry*, edited an introduced by Rita Dove, *The New York Review*, November 24, 2011, https://www.nybooks.com/articles/2011/11/24/are-these-poems-remember.

Rita Dove, "Defending an Anthology," reply to Helen Vendler's review of *The Penguin Anthology of Twentieth-Century American Poetry*, edited an introduced by Rita Dove, *The New York Review*, December 22, 2011, https://www.nybooks.com/articles/2011/12/22/defending-anthology/.

Poetry Foundation, "Rita Dove Defends Anthology in Wake of Helen Vendler Review," Poetry News, December 2, 2011, https://www.poetryfoundation.org/harriet-books/2011/12/rita-dove-defends-anthology-in-wake-of-helen-vendler-review.

AP·PRE·HEN·SION

Neal Whitman, "The Difference Between Homophones, Homonyms, and Homographs," *Business Insider*, September 27, 2015, https://www.businessinsider.com/the-difference-between-homophones-homonyms-and-homographs-2015-9.

AMERICAN LYRIC

William Weir, "A Little Bit Softer Now, a Little Bit Softer Now . . .," *Slate*, September 14, 2014, https://slate.com/culture/2014/09/the-fade-out-in-pop-music-why-dont-modern-pop-songs-end-by-slowly-reducing-in-volume.html.

WAILING MAP

John Spencer Bassett, *Slavery in the State of North Carolina*, electronic ed. (John Hopkins Press, 1899), https://docsouth.unc.edu/nc/bassett99/bassett99.html.

LANDSCAPE WITH MONA LISA

Wikipedia, "*Mona Lisa*," last updated January 17, 2025, https://en.wikipedia.org/wiki/Mona_Lisa.

UNCANNY COLUMBINE

Akshay Singhal, "2D Transformations in Computer Graphics," GateVidyalay, accessed January 23, 2025, https://www.gatevidyalay.com/2d-rotation-in-computer-graphics-definition-examples/.

WE WERE MADE TO PLAY IN THE WHOLENESS OF THE FIELD

Wikipedia, "Electromagnetic Spectrum," last updated December 29, 2024, https://en.wikipedia.org/wiki/Electromagnetic_spectrum.

FIELD SWITCH

"How to Wire a Simple Lighting Circuit," SparkyFacts.co.uk, accessed January 23, 2025, http://www.sparkyfacts.co.uk/Wiring-Diagrams-Simple-Lighting-Circuit.php.

Wikipedia, "Circuit Diagram," last updated January 2, 2025, https://en.wikipedia.org/wiki/Circuit_diagram.

WHO IS THERE TO EULOGIZE THE TREE

Anthony Grafton, *The Footnote: A Curious History* (Harvard University Press, 1999).

{

Anne Carson, *If Not, Winter: Fragments of Sappho* (Knopf Doubleday, 2002).

ACKNOWLEDGMENTS

To Mom, who made a million made-up things with me at the kitchen table. To Dad, for living—and for teaching me to live. To Bryan, for making me laugh harder than anyone else can. To Faye, for taking me on treasure hunts. To Paige, for spinning like a burrito with me. And to Aunt Shawn, who introduced me to poetry and warned me every year—until this one—of the Ides of March.

Poems first appeared in:

The Adroit Journal: "Angles of Incidence" and "Sonnet (Brown)" (published as "How a Brown Sonnet")

The American Poetry Review: "Melting Pot" and "A Transcendental Function" (published as "Transcendental Function: I Hear My Father's Voice, Anesthetized")

The Atlantic: "Batter Bread, Mulatto Style (1935)" (published as "Batter Bread")

Connotation Press: "Uncanny Emmett Till"

Day One: "I Find Myself Defending Pigeons"

December: "Who Is There to Eulogize the Tree"

The Georgia Review: "Spell to Trace a Rainbow to Its Apogee"

The Kenyon Review: "Walmart"

Narrative Magazine: "Muse," "Something Cast from Bronze," and "There's a Concept Called Chronostasis"

New England Review: "The Invitation"

Poetry: "Linedance for an American Textbook" and "Processing Emmett Till" (published as "Processing Emmett Till (Uncanny Emmett Till #2)")

Poems also appeared in:

Machine Dreams and *The Future of Black*: "Uncanny Emmett Till"

Poetry and *Fieldnotes on Ordinary Love*: "I Find Myself Defending Pigeons"

KEITH S. WILSON is a game designer, an Affrilachian poet, and a Cave Canem fellow. He is a recipient of an NEA Fellowship, an Elizabeth George Foundation Grant, and an Illinois Arts Council Agency Award and has received both a Kenyon Review Fellowship and a Wallace Stegner Fellowship. He was a Gregory Djanikian Scholar, and his poetry has won the Rumi Prize and been anthologized in *Best New Poets* and *Best of the Net*. Wilson's *Fieldnotes on Ordinary Love* was recognized by *The New York Times* as a best new book of poetry. He lives in Chicago.

milkweed
EDITIONS

Founded as a nonprofit organization in 1980, Milkweed Editions is an independent publisher. Our mission is to identify, nurture, and publish transformative literature, and build an engaged community around it.

We are based in Bde Óta Othúŋwe (Minneapolis) in Mní Sota Makhóčhe (Minnesota), the traditional homeland of the Dakhóta and Anishinaabe (Ojibwe) people and current home to many thousands of Dakhóta, Ojibwe, and other Indigenous people, including four federally recognized Dakhóta nations and seven federally recognized Ojibwe nations.

We believe all flourishing is mutual, and we envision a future in which all can thrive. Realizing such a vision requires reflection on historical legacies and engagement with current realities. We humbly encourage readers to do the same.

milkweed.org

Milkweed Editions, an independent nonprofit literary publisher, gratefully acknowledges sustaining support from our board of directors, the McKnight Foundation, the National Endowment for the Arts, and many generous contributions from foundations, corporations, and thousands of individuals—our readers. This activity is made possible by the voters of Minnesota through a Minnesota State Arts Board Operating Support grant, thanks to a legislative appropriation from the Arts and Cultural Heritage Fund.

Interior design by Alex Guerra
Typeset in Minion

Minion was designed by Robert Slimbach for Adobe
Systems and released in 1990. He developed Minion to be
used for long passages of body text, taking style influences from
late-Renaissance era type, and adapting it to function
as a classical feeling digital typeface.